SpringerBriefs in Business

For further volumes:
http://www.springer.com/series/8860

Laura Michelini

Social Innovation and New Business Models

Creating Shared Value in Low-Income Markets

Springer

Laura Michelini
Department of Economic and Political
Sciences and Modern Languages
LUMSA University
Rome RM
Italy

ISSN 2191-5482 ISSN 2191-5490 (electronic)
ISBN 978-3-642-32149-8 ISBN 978-3-642-32150-4 (eBook)
DOI 10.1007/978-3-642-32150-4
Springer Heidelberg New York Dordrecht London

Library of Congress Control Number: 2012943628

Printed on acid-free paper

Springer is part of Springer Science+Business Media (www.springer.com)

I would like to acknowledge and thank some people without whom this book would not have been possible
To Professor Iasevoli for his vision, inspiration and guidance
To Daniela Fiorentino for the constructive discussion and suggestions on the case studies analysis
To my colleagues Francesca, Cecilia, Alessandra and Maria for their encouragement and support
To my parents for their unconditional love and never ending support
To my husband Valerio, the sea of my life

Preface

Extreme poverty continues to afflict the world, and it requires urgent action. Along with governments, public institutions, and not-for-profit organizations, currently, companies are playing an important role in facing the world's unsolved social problems.

Social innovation can be the driving force to spark change and to find common ground for shared value creation, specifically when it is directed at low-income markets.

Leading companies have recently developed innovative forms of social innovation by combining three elements—the concept of shared value creation, the theory of the fortune at the bottom of the pyramid, and a corporate social entrepreneurship approach—through which they enter low-income markets by helping to solve global challenges while simultaneously generating profits.

The ultimate objective of this book is to identify the various forms of social innovation with which to target the low-income sector and to describe alternative business models. Moreover, this book aims to identify the main critical success factors for social product innovation.

The first chapter presents an initial overview of the creating shared value approach and the evolution of the bottom of the pyramid theory to identify how companies can generate shared value in low-income markets. The main features of social innovation are identified through an analysis of the recent literature. Finally, the three main levels where social innovation can be performed are identified: alternative business models, new social products, and social communication strategies.

The second chapter analyzes social innovation at the level of the business model. The study clarifies the main characteristics and differences among alternative models of business to target the low-income sector. Starting with the literature on social entrepreneurship and business models, a new theoretical framework "The Social Business Model Framework" is developed. The framework is used to identify the main characteristics of social business models and to emphasize the main area where social innovation can be applied.

In the third chapter—through a literature review of the new product development process and innovation for low-income markets—a new theoretical framework that describes the development process of social products is proposed. By using this social product development framework and a multiple case studies analysis on best practices in social product innovation, this book presents factors that are critical to successfully developing social products for low-income markets. Finally, principles for the communication of social products are proposed.

The last chapter presents a description of four case studies on the social product innovation process: PuR, developed by Procter and Gamble, is a product able to purify water at the household level that is useful for reducing illness in children; Plumpy'nut, developed by Nutriset, is a ready-to-use product for the treatment of severely acute malnutrition; Shokti Doi, developed by Grameen Danone, is a yogurt fortified with calcium, proteins, and micronutrients, which are essential elements for children's growth; Interceptor, developed by BASF, is an insecticide-treated mosquito net that aims to reduce insect-borne diseases, such as malaria.

Contents

Chapter 1
Innovation for Social Change

Abstract The chapter presents an initial overview of the creating shared value approach and the evolution of the bottom of the pyramid theory to identify how companies can generate shared value in low-income markets. The main features of social innovation are identified through an analysis of the recent literature. Finally, the three main levels where social innovation can be performed are identified: alternative business models, new social products and social communication strategies.

Keywords Corporate social responsibility • Creating shared value • Bottom of the pyramid • Social innovation

1.1 The Evolution of Corporate Social Responsibility

Profit making and corporate social responsibility (CSR) have long been considered to be at odds; however, Porter and Kramer (2006, 2011) have recently highlighted the mutual dependence that exists between corporations and society, implying that both business decisions and social policies must follow the principle of creating shared value with choices benefiting both sides. They state that "successful corporations need an healthy society (and) at the same time an healthy society needs successful companies" (Porter and Kramer 2006, p. 83). Companies are increasingly aware that there is an economic perspective to take when helping solve social and environmental problems. They have learned that applying their energies to solving chronic problems found in the social sector powerfully stimulates their own business development. Today's better-educated children will be tomorrow's knowledgeable workers. Lower unemployment in the inner city results in greater inner city consumption. Indeed, a new paradigm for innovation is emerging: a connection between private enterprises and the public interest that produces profitable and sustainable change for both sides. This paradigm is the creating shared value (CSV) approach.

Therefore, from a shared value viewpoint, companies must integrate a social perspective into the core frameworks that they use to understand their competition and to develop their business strategy.

L. Michelini, *Social Innovation and New Business Models*, SpringerBriefs in Business,
DOI: 10.1007/978-3-642-32150-4_1, © The Author(s) 2012

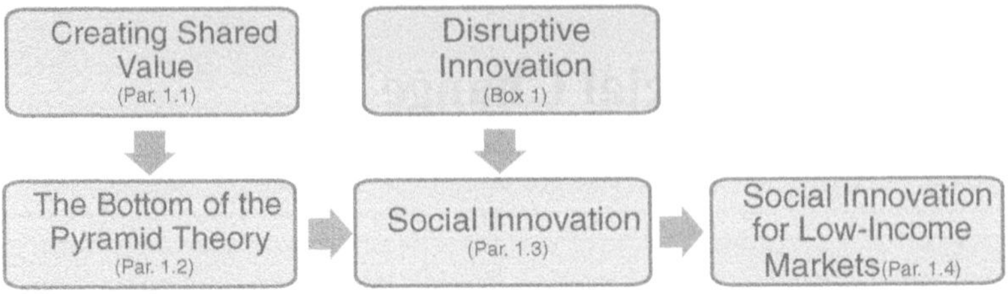

Fig. 1.1 The research process

The shared value principle becomes more influential when companies decide to expand their businesses to developing countries and target the low-income market,[1] where the link between corporations and society grows stronger (Jamali 2010; Matten and Crane 2005). In fact, on the one hand, these countries represent a good business opportunity and, on the other hand, they are characterized by substantial social problems. Thus, corporate social responsibility strategies should generate profit, as well as social value to a greater degree than in other markets (Michelini and Fiorentino 2012).

Following Porter and Kramer's theory, companies that have already invested or want to invest in developing countries have a choice of corporate social responsibility strategies. First, they could reduce the dangers caused by their value chain. Second, they might choose a philanthropic strategy that improves the most important areas of their competitive context. Finally, they might opt to create a shared value approach where the social dimension of their strategy becomes part of the value proposition.

In the third case, Porter and Kramer note that "the concept of shared value blurs the line between for-profit and nonprofit organizations. New kinds of hybrid enterprises are rapidly appearing" (p. 67, 2011). Recently, for-profit companies, engaging in strategic CSR, have chosen to implement new hybrid business models that are part of the broader trend of studies in the corporate social entrepreneurship school of thought (Austin et al. 2005).

Companies are, therefore, reassessing their business models to create new business opportunities in which they approach the low-income market by helping solve global challenges while simultaneously generating profits.

Several leading companies are beginning the transition from the pursuit of corporate social responsibility to the development of corporate social entrepreneurship (CSE) processes. Moreover, Kanter (1999) uses the term "corporate social innovation" to assert that firms should use social issues as learning laboratories to identify unmet needs and to develop solutions. Corporate social innovation is an important approach for companies that decide to reach the low-income market (Mahlouji and Anaraki 2009).

This chapter presents an initial overview of the bottom of the pyramid theory to identify how to create shared value in low-income markets. The characteristics of social innovation will be analyzed and then the main dimensions of social innovation for low-income markets will be presented (Fig. 1.1).

[1] Other authors' use of the term "low-income community" (LIC) can be considered synonymous with low-income market.

1.2 The Bottom of the Pyramid Theory

Currently, companies are faced with a competitive, global scenario characterized by opposing dynamics. On the one hand, in industrialized countries, many people are willing to pay high price for certain products and services. On the other hand, the basic needs of millions of people in non-industrialized countries remain unmet because this population of potential customers is considered unable to provide compensation for products and services that would satisfy these needs. It is within this dynamic that the debate between the impact of the business internationalization process and the role of corporate social responsibility strategies takes place. However, the apparent incompatibility between these two dynamics progressively disappears because of the integration of the international economic environment's evolution with a theoretical and practical analysis of sustainable development. Internationalization can be developed in three ways (Bartlett and Ghoshal 1989; Porter 1990):

- the expansion of mercantile, products manufactured in the original country are exported and sold abroad;
- the intermediate forms of internationalization, such as agreements, licenses, contracts and commercial technical support to allow companies to sell or lease the technology to local operators of foreign countries, and;
- foreign direct investment (FDI), in which the multinational enterprise (MNE) owns production facilities in one or more foreign countries, possibly in joint ventures with local operators (considering both majority-owned and minority-owned shares). Character qualifying FDI reflects the fact that the foreign investors are directly involved in the governance and management of companies in which they hold an equity stake and can therefore significantly affect strategic and operational decisions.

Occasionally, in the internationalization process, a company takes on a new form of "corporate imperialism" (Prahalad and Lieberthal 1998, 2003), a term which refers to companies who market their products to a small segment of relatively affluent buyers in developing countries. The result of this approach, as Prahalad remarks, is that companies have missed the very real opportunity to reach larger markets further down the socioeconomic pyramid.

In the early 2000s, Prahalad published two articles and a book: "The Fortune at the Bottom of the Pyramid" (2002), in *Strategy + Business* with S. Hart, "Serve the World's Poor, Profitably" (2002) in the *Harvard Business Review* with Hammond and "The Fortune at the Bottom of the Pyramid" (2004).

Prahalad coined the term "Bottom of the Pyramid" (BOP), recognizing that 4 billion people in the world live with a per capita income below $2 a day. He highlighted the fact that this population can be considered a potential market. This target can also be referred more generally as the low-income market.

The real power of these studies is that they alter perception of the poor. Poor are people not only to help but also to serve. People living in poverty can be considered a market to target with specific products and services. This approach is based on the concept that business can play a key role in eradicating poverty.

Prahalad argues that markets at the bottom of the economic pyramid are fundamentally new sources of growth for multinational companies. Growth can be extremely rapid, because these markets are in the earliest stage of development.

The Organization for Economic Co-operation and Development (OECD) Report (2011) argues the emergence of a new phenomenon called "shifting wealth", wherein the center of the economic gravity of the world has progressively shifted from west to east and from north to south, resulting in a new geography of growth. Over the last decade, developing countries, in general, have enjoyed their economic fortune after nearly 20 years of missed opportunities and disappointing performance. The 2000s were the first time in many decades that poorer developing countries grew at a faster rate than high income economies: as many as 83 developing countries managed to double OECD per capita growth rates, thereby increasing the number of converging countries. Today, nearly 1 billion of the world's 2 billion people living on $10 to $100 (USD) a day—the global middle class—live in converging countries. This number is expected to exceed more than 3 billion in 2030.

In this scenario, some global companies have turned their attention to emerging countries (such as China, Brazil and India) and developing countries (such as Bangladesh), looking for wider growing low-income markets.

Conversely, developed economies experience increasingly critical situations. Poverty rates for 2010 rose higher than 22 % of the population in five European countries (Greece, Portugal, Italy, Spain and the United Kingdom), In Italy, in 2010, the percentage of families living in relatively poor conditions was 11 %. Greece, Portugal and Spain (where there are more than 11 million people living in poverty) also have worrying rates of serious material deprivation (Source: ISTAT 2011).

Many studies have shown that companies' attempts have not been successful because of an inability to attract customers in the low-income market with rewarding marketing strategies. Specifically, Deloitte Touche Tohmatsu (2006) reports that long term success in emerging markets depends on innovative product offerings and not on micro adjustments to existing products, lowering prices or new sales channels. According to market research, over 80 % of the products sold in emerging markets were the same or slightly different from the products sold in the home markets.

When the surveyed companies modified their product offerings, they were more likely to adjust the pricing or the discount or rebate policy (or both), rather than to offer fundamentally different product features or types to appeal to the unique profile of emerging market customers (Fig. 1.2). The study underlined that "emerging markets are becoming the catalyst for new product and service innovation. But tapping the talent and growth potential of these rising economies will require manufacturers to shed many of their assumptions about customer needs, product design, and innovation strategies that they have relied upon in the developed economies" (Deloitte Touche Tohmatsu 2006, p. 4).

Stressing Prahalad's position on serving the poor without exploitation and following his remarks that in the rush to capture the fortune at the bottom of the pyramid "the perspective of the poor themselves" has been lost, Simanis and Hart (2008) proposed the BOP protocol, second edition (or BOP 2.0 as it is more commonly known). The protocol presents a strategic framework that organizations can

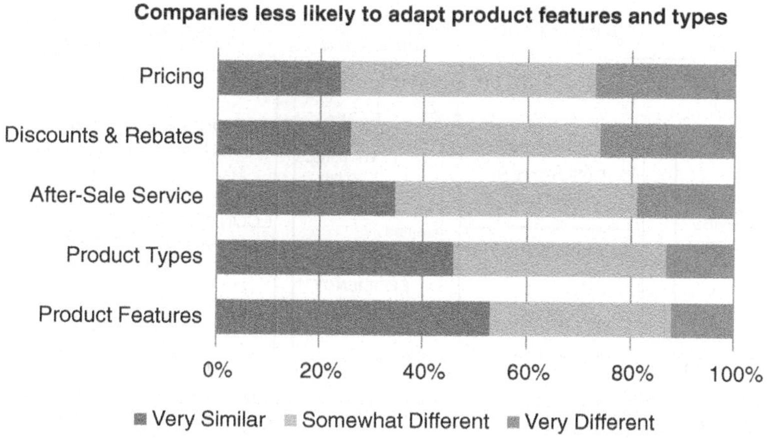

Fig. 1.2 Companies product adaptation in emerging and home markets. *Source* Deloitte Touche Tohmatsu (2006)

use to successfully engage the bottom of the pyramid. According to the authors, it is imperative that companies move rapidly to a "second-generation" of corporate BOP strategies that go beyond mere deep listening and extend into a deep dialogue with the poor that will result in a shared commitment born out of a mutual learning experience. The second-generation BOP strategy "requires an embedded process of co-invention and co-creation that brings corporations into close, personal business partnerships with BOP communities" (Simanis and Hart 2008, p. 2).

A further analysis by Sánchez and Ricart (2010) identifies two types of business model configurations that can be implemented to reach the low-income market:

- *isolated* business models are characterized by an exploitation strategy, which leverages the firm's own resources and capabilities for seeking efficiency;
- *interactive* business models are characterized by an exploration strategy, which leverages on external resources and fosters learning and innovation processes.

An isolated business model acts as an efficiency seeker's model, and the strategy is based on the possibilities of increasing the firm's global market share through product adaptation and the optimization of business processes. Thus, the firm individually replicates and extends its traditional business model, adapting it to the ecosystem's contextual conditions with the aim of achieving the highest possible efficiency in its operations. Different interactive business models are mainly focused on learning and innovating, and the value created emerges from the right combination of firm's resources and capabilities with those of the ecosystem.

Sánchez and Ricart (2010) conclude that the logic of value creation in the low-income market depends on the nature of the business model. Figure 1.3 presents the different source of value creation in the two business models. In the context of the isolated business model, the aim of the company is to increase efficiency by reducing costs and fixing the price below the level that consumers are willing to

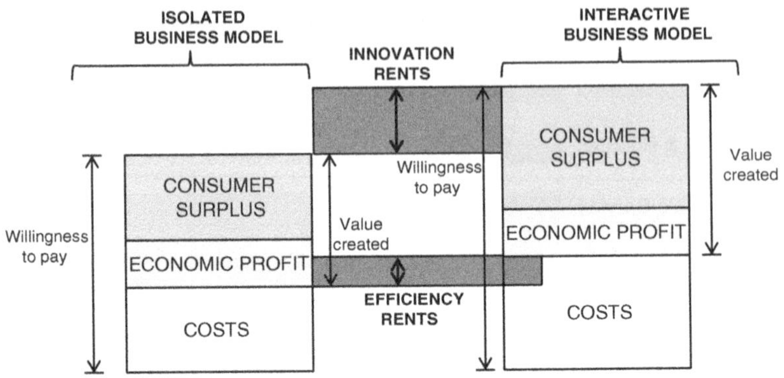

Fig. 1.3 Source of value creation in isolated and interactive business models. Adapted by: Sáncheze and Ricart (2010)

pay. In the case of the interactive business model, the company aims to generate innovations that increase the willingness to pay by enhancing the value created for customers as well as enhancing customers' capacity to pay.

Prahalad has argued for a reconsideration of the elements of the BOP business model (Prahalad and Lieberthal 1998, 2003). Several authors, moreover, have suggested ideas and approaches and given useful advice for succeeding in low-income sectors. The critical issues that companies must address can be summarized as follows (Deloitte 2006; Prahalad and Lieberthal 1998, 2003; Chandra and Neelankavil 2008):

- *rethinking the price/performance equation* because consumers are more price sensitive. Rethinking the equation means not simply cutting off costs in product development but creating new products at a lower price. Having a lower cost does not necessarily mean having less quality or less sophistication. Developing additional benefits for traditional products is necessary to satisfy specific market needs while maintaining a low price level. To better understand the needs of the low-income segment, companies must invest the necessary resources to gain a deep understanding of these needs. Each country is unique, and the needs within a single country can vary widely;
- *adapting the brand strategy to the local market*;
- *rethinking the costs of market building*, considering that altering regional habits is difficult and expensive;
- *globalizing R&D*, which means not only reducing expenses and obtaining governments incentives but also, to have an even greater effect, incorporating local needs and expertise into product design;
- *planning new distribution strategies*, adapting marketing and sales strategies;
- *combining expatriates and local executives,* which helps the company to capture global knowledge while considering local sensitivities (providing opportunities for professional growth and advancement is critical);
- *managing the joint venture* with local partners and considering partners' expectations.

Table 1.1 The evolution of the BOP theory

Pillars	Business model building blocks	BOP 1.0	BOP 2.0	Sources
Product	Value proposition	Adaptation	Value added	Deloitte Touche Tohmatsu (2006), Chandra and Neelankavil (2008)
Customer interface	Target customer	Poor as consumers	Poor as business partners	Simanis and Hart (2008), Perrot (2011)
	Distribution channel	Extend distribution	Build shared commitment	Deloitte Touche Tohmatsu (2006), Prahalad and Lieberthal (1998, 2003)
	Relationship	Listening	Dialogue	Simanis and Hart (2008)
Infrastructure management	Value configuration	Isolated	Co-creation; mutual value	Prahalad and Lieberthal (1998, 2003), Brugmann and Prahalad (2007)
	Core competency	Existing knowledge	New capabilities	Sánchez and Ricart (2010)
	Partner network	Arm's length relationships mediating by NGOs	Direct, relationships facilitated by NGOs	Simanis and Hart (2008)
Financial aspects	Cost structure	Efficiency	Innovation	Sánchez and Ricart (2010)
	Revenue model	Profit	Profit and hybrid	Porter and Kramer (2011

The theory of the fortune at the bottom of the pyramid has evolved over time as a result of the contributions of many scholars. Starting from existing literature, we have analyzed the evolution of the theory from the BOP 1.0 to the BOP 2.0 by employing Osterwalder and Pigneur's (2010) theoretical framework for analyzing business models.

Table 1.1 summarizes the evolution of these business models (for further information on the business model literature see Chap. 2). Finally, both approaches can coexist, and choosing one over another is dependent on market characteristics (Perrot 2011).

The second generation of this theory stresses the importance of adding value to the product. BOP 2.0 strategies, then, view the poor not exclusively as consumers, but as business partners, and the relationship extends beyond mere listening to a deep dialogue. This relationship between the company and the community is direct and it is not mediated but facilitated by an NGO.

Distribution channel strategies are based on the concept of a shared business commitment that entails value co-creation and stresses the importance of involving local partners and sharing a vision and sense of responsibility.

In terms of the value configuration, the concept of mutual value means that each step of the process creates value for all partners, while the co-creation process captures the need for the company to work in equal partnership with the low-income community to launch and grow a sustainable business.

Under BOP 2.0, the company's main financial aim is not only to increase production efficiency to reduce costs but also to innovate the production process itself. This revenue model can be analyzed not only by considering the way a company makes money through a variety of revenue flows, but also by examining revenue management. From this perspective, the evolution of the BOP theory shows that the line between for-profit and not-for-profit models is becoming blurred and that new kinds of hybrid enterprises are rapidly appearing (Porter and Kramer 2011). These kinds of enterprises can be analyzed starting from the broader trend of studies of the corporate social entrepreneurship (Austin et al. 2005).

In conclusion, following the BOP theory proposed by Prahalad (2004), which is based on the concept of "serving the poor profitably", it is now evident that profitability in LIC could only be achieved if companies change their traditional opinions toward developing countries by no longer regarding them as territories to exploit but as uncharted territories (or as entirely different markets) characterized by good producers and good consumers with specific needs, which in turn could be satisfied through specific and innovative businesses (Austin et al. 2007). Importantly, it is necessary to "turn LIC into partners" (Marwaha et al. 2005), as doing so could result in profits for both the company and the LIC. BOP scholars often argue that, to be successful, solutions must be co-created by the exogenous actors and the poor.

Prahalad (2011) notes that the new challenge in the BOP market is to "convert the unorganized and fragmented markets to an organized, private sector market" (p. 6), thereby converting the bottom of the pyramid to microconsumers, microproducers, microinvestors, and innovators. BOP allows companies to explore the possibility of an unreached market of new microconsumers and microproducers, but the emphasis should be switched from a product-centric approach to a focus on business model innovation, from which the product is derived (Prahalad 2011).

Moreover, Prahalad states that a new perspective is emerging, and "many global firms are increasingly using the BOP markets as a laboratory for innovation not only for the BOP markets but also for the established country markets" (2011, p. 11). He concludes by wondering: "if a cheap car, compliant with European standards of emissions, is sold in India, why could it not be sold in Europe?" Thus, he highlights a new paradigm of development that starts from the innovation of the BOP market and a "move toward the middle class" to achieve global competitiveness. Concerning the replicability of the model, it has always been focused on poor or developing countries, because of the belief that advanced economies do not need to have this type of business formula. Yet, in analyzing trends in the number of people living below the poverty line in Europe, we discover that over 15 % of the population lives in conditions of great hardship and on the margins of society in many countries.

1.3 What Is Social Innovation?

Innovation is recognized to play a central role in creating value and sustaining a competitive advantage and it is considered to be the "life blood of corporate survival and growth" (Zahara and Covin 1994, p. 183). As long ago as 1950, Schumpeter argued that organizations should innovate to renew the value of their asset endowment. But what is innovation? Is it a new idea? Is it a new process? In the academic literature there are different approaches to defining the concept of innovation. One of the early definitions was proposed by Thompson (1965, p. 2), who affirmed that "innovation is the generation, acceptance and implementation of new ideas, processes, products or services". For some authors, innovation is concerned with the practical application and commercialization of ideas or inventions. Thus, innovation is expressed by the following equation: theoretical conception + technical invention + commercial exploitation. The conception refers to the new idea, the invention is the new artifact (mainly a product or process), and exploitation is to complete the process through the commercialization (Trott 2008). Innovation has been more simply defined as "new ideas that work" (Mulgan 2006). Therefore, social innovation refers to new ideas that work in meeting social goals. Social innovation is, thereby, considered a vehicle that creates social change that is related to a better quality of life and that develops solutions and approaches to various sets of problems.

The notion of social innovation has been analyzed by different authors, and several approaches toward this concept may be distinguished (see Table 1.2).

Some researchers focus on the social consequences of innovation and highlight the fact that social innovation is by the aim of satisfy social needs or solve social problem (Christensen et al. 2006; Mulgan et al. 2007; Phills et al. 2008).

Other researchers primarily stress the fact that social innovation is sustainability-driven innovation (Little 2006; Bisgaard 2009) that uses social, environmental or sustainable motivations to create new ways of working, new products, services, processes and new markets. According to this perspective, social innovation is defined as innovation that adds value to a business, its customers, the environment and society (Confederation of Indian Industry—Centre of Excellence for Sustainable Development, CII-ITC CESD 2010). Social innovation is not defined by the introduction of new types of production, or by the exploitation of new markets. It does, however, include the satisfaction of new needs that are not met by the market and the creation of new, more satisfactory ways of giving people a place and a role in production (OECD 2010).

The well-being of society is explicitly highlighted by Pol and Ville (2009), who pointed out that social innovation should improve either the quality or the quantity of life.[2] Therefore, social innovation should allow people to achieve better education, better environmental quality and longer life expectancy.

---

[2] The authors refer, in particular, to macro-quality of life issues (versus micro-level issues that regard a specific individual). The determinants of the quality of life are material well-being, education opportunities (including quality of teaching and learning practices), health domain, job security, family life, community life, environment (climate and geography), political freedom, political stability and security, and gender equality (Pol and Ville 2009, p. 882).

Table 1.2 Main definitions of social innovation

Source and year	Definition
Social Innovation Europe (2012)	Social innovations are new ideas, institutions, or ways of working that meet social needs more effectively (than existing approaches).
Organization for Economic Co-operation and Development (OECD) (2010)	Social innovation deals with improving the welfare of individuals and communities through employment, consumption or participation, its expressed purpose being to provide solutions for individual and community problem.
CII-ITC CESD (2010)	Sustainable and inclusion innovation concerns innovations that add value to business, to customers, to the environment and to society.
Pol and Ville (2009)	An innovation is expressed as social innovation if the implied new idea has the potential to improve either the quality or the quantity of life.
Bisgaard (2009)	New products, services, business models, processes, distribution channels and so on are able to solve global challenges related to both environmental issues and social problems.
Phills et al. (2008)	A novel solution to a social problem that is more effective, efficient, sustainable, or just than existing solutions and for which the value created accrues primarily to society, as a whole, rather than private individuals.
Mulgan (2006), Mulgan et al. (2007)	Social innovation is new ideas that work in meeting social goals. Innovative activities and services that are motivated by the goal of meeting a social need and that are predominantly developed and diffused through organizations whose primary purposes are social.
Christensen et al. (2006)	Social innovation is subset of disruptive innovations whose primary objective is social change.
Little (2006)	Social innovation is the use of social, environmental or sustainability drivers to create new ways of working, new products, services and processes, and new market space.

Christensen et al. (2006) defined social innovation as a "catalytic innovation" and considered it to be a new subset of disruptive innovation (see Box 1) that is based on social change. Like disruptive innovation, which offers simple and good alternatives to an underserved group of customers, catalytic innovation can improve the status quo by providing sufficient solutions to insufficiently addressed social problems.

Disruptive innovations have had a significant effect on industry structures and have often resulted in social change. However, the social changes caused by disruptive innovations are largely unintended; they are simply the by-products of pursuing business opportunities, while in catalytic innovation the social change is the main goal.

According to Christensen et al. (2006) catalytic innovators have five primary qualities:

- they create systemic social change through scaling and replication;
- they meet a need that is either over-served (because the existing solution is more complex than many people require) or not served at all;
- they offer products and services that are simpler and less costly than existing alternatives and may be perceived as having a lower level of performance, but users consider them to be sufficient;
- they generate resources, such as donations, grants, volunteer manpower or intellectual capital, in ways that are initially unattractive to incumbent competitors;
- they are often ignored, disparaged, or even encouraged by existing players for whom the business model is unprofitable or otherwise unattractive and who, therefore, avoid or retreat from the market segment.

Box 1—The disruptive innovation model

The disruptive innovation model was introduced by Christensen and Raynor (2003) and it identifies some critical aspects of product innovation evident in three types of product performance: performance demanded by customers, the sustaining innovation and the disruptive innovation.

The first critical aspect is inherent the product's performance level that customers demanded and their ability to utilize the new product's improvements.

The sustaining innovation indicates the typical pace of innovation and the improvement of the product undertaken by firms. Sustaining innovation generally gives existing customers more than they need or are actually able to use. This pace of product advancement nearly always outstrips mainstream customers' abilities to benefit from the improvement.

The second critical component of the model is the difference between sustaining and disruptive innovations. Sustaining innovation provide better quality or additional functionality for the attractive customer with the willingness to pay a high price. In contrast, disruptive innovations are related neither to already satisfied customers' needs nor to already existing products or services. Because disruptive innovations are typically 1) simpler, 2) more convenient, and 3) less expensive, they appeal to new or less demanding customers.

Christensen and Raynor also add that there are two types of disruptive innovations: those targeting new customers and those addressing the low-income market with low-cost products. Both of these types have profit as their sole and primary purpose.

Table 1.3 The 7 + 1 features of social innovation

The features of social innovation
1 It must generate a positive social impact
2 It is driven by both social and economic motivations
3 It must be novel
4 It can be promoted by different actors (businesses, NGO, public institution, etc.)
5 It must be scalable
6 It must be sustainable
7 It can take different forms
+1 It must improve and change the lives of the poor

Social innovation's main features were identified by starting with a literature analysis to capture the common denominators of existing definitions.

These features are described in Table 1.3. The first feature of social innovation is the *social goal.* Innovation is one of the main drivers that affects economic growth and that improves the standard of living. Social innovation is a vehicle to create social change, increase the quality of life, and develop solutions and approaches to various sets of problems.

The social impact of innovation is concerned with (CII-ITC CESD 2010):

- increasing the quality of life of the people beyond the immediate use of the product or service;
- creating a product or service of an uncompromising quality at a price that is affordable, and;
- addressing the challenge of resource use efficiency to manage drastically low cost structures.

It is also important to emphasize that the social impact of innovations on the community is twofold (Butkevičienė 2009): social innovations are shaped by the social system (e.g., the legal framework, the actors involved in the innovation development process) and, at the same time, are influencing the social system.

The second feature directly linked with the social impact of innovation is the *motivation* that leads to social innovation. Business innovations are generally motivated by profit and diffused through organizations that are primarily motivated by profit maximization. However, there are many situations where the lines are blurred; for example, for-profit businesses may innovate by developing new approaches to assist the disabled in the workplace (Mulgan 2006).

Different motivations lead to different forms of organizations (see Fig. 1.4). Profit is the main motivation of the traditional business, social motivation represents the nature of not-for-profit and public organizations, and profit and social motivation create new hybrid forms of enterprise (see also Chap. 2).

Our approach considers that social innovation refers to innovations that are social and inclusive in nature, independently from the motivation (profit or not-for-profit).

The third aspect is the *novelty*. Although innovations do not need to be original, they must be new to the user, the context, or the application. Hence, novelty can take the following different, new forms: ideas, activities, products,

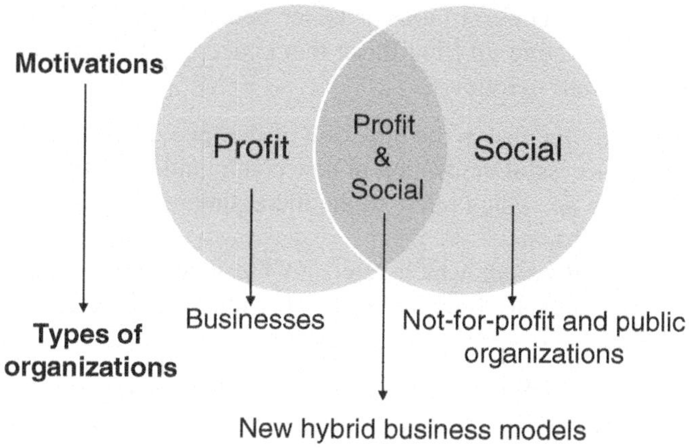

Fig. 1.4 Motivations and types of organizations of social innovation

services, business models, processes or distribution channels. To gain a real competitive advantage, the main aim of the innovation must be to develop products that are new for the world, or for the market, and to be able to convince consumers that they will receive a new benefit from the product. This process entails a new way or manner of considering an existing idea or knowledge. New social ideas are rarely entirely new in themselves. More commonly, they combine ideas that had previously been separate (Mulgan 2006). Social innovation often "involves not just new ideas but the remaking and reuse of existing ideas" (SIE 2012, p. 17).

The fourth characteristic is related to the *actors* that promote social innovation. Social innovation can be driven by governments, private sector, civil society or a combination of these actors. The Social Innovation Europe[3] (SIE) notes that "social innovation can and must come from all sectors—the public sector, the private market, the third sector, and individuals/household—and that many innovations move between sectors as they evolve" (SIE 2012, p. 19). Innovation can also be suggested and developed by global actors, for example multinational corporations or a large domestic company (top-down approach) or by a local actor (a bottom-up approach). Furthermore, an external actor can facilitate a local institution's capacity to be able to mobilize resources and develop social innovation (top-down innovation to facilitate bottom-up activity), (Butkevičienė 2009).

Social innovation must also be *scalable*. The concept of scaling up refers to increasing the scope or reach of an activity, program, project, or initiative so that it

[3] The Social Innovation Europe initiative (SIE) is a project run by a consortium of partners including Euclid Network, the Danish Technological Institute and the Young Foundation and led by the Social Innovation eXchange (SIX). It was funded by the European Commission's DG Enterprise and Industry.

serves more people or delivers more or better benefits (UNDP 2008). There are different models of scaling up,[4] but those that concern the developmental impact of social innovation are as follows:

- *qualitative scaling up*, that is the diffusion of the innovation, which can involve replicating the successful innovation in new communities or cover a larger area;
- *functional scaling up*, which refers to the increasing of typologies of innovation (e.g., diversification), and;
- *organizational scaling up,* which refers to the increasing of efficiency (e.g., improving management system of the organizations) of the innovation's promoter.

Additionally, social innovation must be *sustainable*, meaning that it must meet economic and environmental challenges. Social innovation must be economically sustainable and, at the same time, minimize harmful effects on the environment that are caused by its development and diffusion, and it must achieve continual improvement of its environmental performance.

Finally, social innovation can take *different forms*. According to the European Union definition (2012) social innovations can be "a new service, initiative or organization, or, alternatively, a radically new approach to the organization and delivery of services. Social innovations can also spread in the form of ideas, values, software, tools and habits. Innovations in all of these senses can spread throughout a profession or sector, such as education or healthcare, or geographically from one place to another" (p. 17).

The social value of social innovation takes on greater importance when it involves or is directed at poor people. Innovation that targets the low-income market is known as "sustainable & inclusive innovation (SI2)", (CII-ITC CESD 2010). SI2 concerns innovation that faces two challenges: poverty and environmental damage.

To simplify the definition and avoid confusion with using different terms, the general expression "social innovation for the low-income market" will be used.

Social innovation for the low-income market is innovation that has the central aim of improving and changing the lives and well-being of the poor; it can be referred to as an idea, process, product or service. It must possess the 7 + 1 features.

To better understand the concept of well-being, Table 1.4 outlines its main elements. Poverty is caused by the lack of some, or all, of the elements of human well-being. These elements begin with sufficient income to obtain adequate food and shelter; however, other dimensions of well-being are also important, such as good health, security, social acceptance, access to opportunity, and freedom of choice (UNDP 2008).

---

[4] The models are qualitative, functional, organizational, political (increasing the political power of an organization or enterprise) and institutional (referring to growing the public institution necessary for establishing and distributing the benefits of ecosystem enterprises) (UNDP 2008).

Table 1.4 Elements of well-being. *Source* Millennium Ecosystem Assessment (2005)

Elements of well-being	
Physical and Financial Necessities	Adequate Livelihood Sufficient Nutritious Food Shelter Access to Goods
Health	Strength and Fitness for Activity Feeling Well Access to Clean Air and Water
Security	Personal Safety Secure Resource Access Security from Disasters
Good Social Relations	Social Cohesion Mutual Respect Ability to Help Others
Freedom of Choice and Action	Opportunity to Achieve What an Individual Values Doing and Being

1.4 Social Innovation for Low-Income Markets

In conclusion, the integration of Christensen's disruptive-innovation model with Prahalad's (2004) BOP theory and the creating share value approach maintained by Porter and Kramer (2006) has created a new and important field of research: social innovation for the low-income market.

These theories and the subsequent literature that they have produced have highlighted the importance of carefully managing this type of innovation by using managerial and entrepreneurial tools that allow us to increase the well-being of this target sector.

Academic literature argues that there are different typologies of innovations (Trott 2008; Schilling 2008):

- product innovation, which is concerned with the development of a new or improved product;
- process innovation, which reflects changes in how a company operates;
- organizational innovation, which is concerned with changes in the organizational structure and can refer to a new venture division;
- management innovation, which can be concerned with, for example, the implementation of a Total Quality Management System; and
- commercial/marketing innovation, which is concerned with innovation in the marketing strategies and mix.

In particular, social innovation for the low-income market can refer to three main dimensions: business model, product and process, and diffusion/communication (see Fig. 1.5).

First, innovation can concern an alternative model of business. Alternative models of business address specific perceived shortcomings in more mainstream

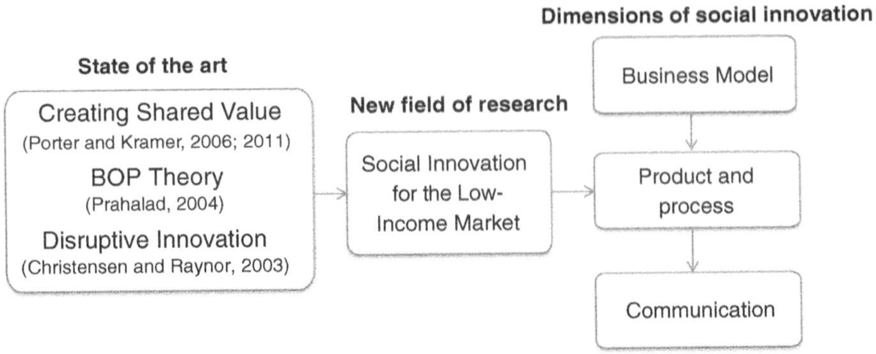

Fig. 1.5 The three dimensions of social innovation for the low-income market

models, for example, around ownership and control; the distribution of residual earnings or profits; objectives, motivations and incentives toward multiple bottom lines; the quality of working practices; or alterations in the terms of trade. Innovative business models can generate different types of enterprises as new age enterprises, social enterprises, community-based enterprises, hybrid organizations and inclusive businesses (Westall 2007; CII-ITC CESD 2010).

With this in mind, Christensen et al. (2006) note the importance of assessing the business model, stating that "just because an organization has come up with a good idea for systemic social change does not mean that it will succeed in implementing that change. At this third stage in the evaluation of a potential innovation, assess whether the group's business model can allow it not only to effectively introduce the innovation but also to scale it up and sustain it" (p. 101).

Thus, the focus of innovation should be to switch from a product-centric approach to a focus on business model innovation, from which the product descends (Prahalad 2011). Moreover, serving the BOP means providing products and services that have specific value.

Finally, innovation can refer to the way in which an idea, a product or a service can be spread. It is the process by which an innovation is adopted and gains acceptance by members of a particular community (Surry 1997).

References

Austin J, Leonard H, Reficco E, Wei-Skillem J (2005) Social entrepreneurship: it's for corporations, too. In: Nicholls A (ed) Social entrepreneurship: new paradigms of sustainable social change, Oxford University Press, Oxford

Austin J, Marques P, Reficco E (2007) Building new value chains with low income sectors in Latin America. In: Rangan V, Quelch J, Herrero G, Barton B (eds) Business solutions for the global poor: creating social and economic value, Jossey-Bass, San Francisco

Bartlett CA, Ghoshal S (1989) Managing across borders. Harvard Business School Press, Boston

Bisgaard T (2009) Corporate social innovation. Companies' participation in solving global challenges. http://www.ebst.dk/publikationer/Corporate_Social_Innovation/pdf/CSI_Report_web.pdf. Accessed 16 May 2012

Brugmann J, Prahalad CK (2007) Cocreating business's new social compact. Harvard Business Review, Boston, pp 80–90

Butkevičienė E (2009) Social innovations in rural communities: methodological framework and empirical evidence. Soc Sci 1:80–88

Chandra M, Neelankavil JP (2008) Product development and innovation for developing countries. J Manag Dev 10:1017–1025

Christensen CM, Raynor ME (2003) The innovator's solution: creating and sustaining successful growth. Harvard Business School Press, Boston

Christensen CM, Baumann H, Ruggles R, Sadtler TM (2006) Disruptive innovation for social change. Harvard Business Review, Boston, pp 94–101

CII-ITC CESD (2010) Sustainable and inclusive innovation strategies for tomorrow's world, crossmedia solutions. http://www.sustainabledevelopment.in/publications/downloads/SUSTAINABLE_INCLUSIVE_INNOVATION_24nov.pdf. Accessed 11 May 2012

Deloitte Touche Tohmatsu (2006) Laboratories of Innovation: Leveraging Emerging Markets for Commercial Success. http://www.deloitte.com/assets/Dcom-Albania/Local %20Assets/Documents/dtt_manufacturing_laboratories_of_innovation(1).pdf. Accessed 11 May 2012

European Union (2012) Financing social impact. Funding social innovation in Europe –mapping the way forward. http://ec.europa.eu/enterprise/newsroom/cf/_getdocument.cfm?doc_id=7048. Accessed 15 May 2012

Jamali D (2010) CSR of MNC subsidiaries in developing countries: global, local, substantive or diluted? J Bus Ethics 93:181–200

Kanter RM (1999) From spare change to real change. Harvard Business Review, Boston May–June:122–132

Little AD (2006) The innovation high ground: Winning tomorrow's customers using sustainability-driven innovation. Strateg Dir 1:35–37

Mahlouji H, Anaraki NK (2009) Corporate social responsibility towards social responsible innovation: a dynamic capability approach. Int Rev Bus Res Pap 6:185–194

Marwaha K, Kulkarni A, Mukophadyay J, Sivakuma S (2005) IBENEX: Business effectiveness—the next level: being served by the poor. In: Paper presented at HBS Global Poverty Conference 1–3 December

Matten D, Crane A (2005) Corporate citizenship: toward an extended theoretical conceptualisation. Acad Manag Rev 30:166–179

Michelini L, Fiorentino D (2012) New business models for creating shared value. Soc Responsib J, 8 (Forthcoming)

Millennium Ecosystem Assessment (2005) Ecosystems and Human well-being: desertification synthesis. Washington: World Resources Institute. http://www.millenniumassessment.org/documents/document.355.aspx.pdf. Accessed 11 May 2012

Mulgan G (2006) The process of social innovation innovations: technology governance. Globalization 2:145–162

Mulgan G, Tucker S, Ali R, Sander B (2007) Social innovation: what it is, why it matters and how it can be accelerated. Said Business School, Oxford

Organization for Economic Co-operation and Development (OECD) (2010) SMEs, Entrepreneurship and Innovation. http://www.oecd.org/document/16/0,3746,en_2649_33956792_44938128_1_1_1_1,00.html. Accessed 11 May 2012

Organization for Economic Co-operation and Development (OECD) Report (2011) Perspectives on Global Development. Social Cohesion in a Shifting World. http://www.oecd.org/site/0,3407,en_21571361_49041236_1_1_1_1_1,00.html. Accessed 11 May 2012

Osterwalder A, Pigneur Y (2010) Business model generation. Wiley, Hoboken

Perrott F. (2011) Multinational corporations at the base of the economic pyramid: a strategic analysis framework. PhD Dissertation, Ecole Polytechnique, Paris

Phills JA, Deiglmeier K, Miller DT (2008) Rediscovering social innovation. Stanf Soc Innov Rev 6:34–43
Pol E, Ville S (2009) Social innovation: buzz word or enduring term? J Socio-Econ 6:878–885
Porter ME (1990) The competitive advantage of nations. Free Press, New York
Porter ME, Kramer MR (2006) Strategy and society. The link between competitive advantage and corporate social responsibility. Harv Bus Rev 84(12):78–92
Porter ME, Kramer MR (2011) Creating shared value. Harv Bus Rev 89(1):62–77
Prahalad CK (2004) The fortune at the bottom of the pyramid: eradicating poverty with profits. Wharton Business Publishing, Philadelphia
Prahalad CK (2011) Bottom of the pyramid as a source of breakthrough innovations. J Prod Innov Manage 1:6–12
Prahalad CK, Lieberthal K (1998) The end of corporate imperialism. Harv Bus Rev 4:68–79 (Reprinted in Harvard Business Review August 2003)
Prahalad CK, Lieberthal K (2003) The end of corporate imperialism. Reprinted in Harvard Business Review August 109–117
Sánchez P, Ricart E (2010) Business model innovation and sources of value creation in low-income markets. Eur Manag Rev 7:138–154
Schilling MA (2008) Strategic management of technological innovation, 2nd edn. The McGraw Hill Companies
Simanis E, Hart S (2008) The base of the pyramid protocol: toward next generation BoP strategy. http://www.stuartlhart.com/sites/stuartlhart.com/files/BoPProtocol2ndEdition2008_0.pdf. Accessed 11 May 2012
Social Innovation Europe (2012), Financing Social Impact. http://ec.europa.eu/enterprise/newsroom/cf/itemdetail.cfm?item_id=5582&lang=en. Accessed 11 May 2012
Surry DW (1997) Diffusion theory and instructional technology. In: Proceedings of the annual conference of the association for educational communications and technology (University of Southern Mississippi): Albuquerque, New Mexico, February: 12–15
Thompson VA (1965) Bureaucracy and innovation. Adm Sci Q 10:1–20
Trott P (2008) Innovation management and new product development. Financial Times Prentice Hall, New Jersey
Westall A (2007) How can innovation in social enterprise be understood, encouraged and enabled? http://www.cabinetoffice.gov.uk/upload/assets/www.cabinetoffice.gov.uk/third_sector/innovation_social_enterprise.pdf. Accessed 16 May 2012
United Nations Development Programme (UNDP) (2008) Creating value for all: strategies for doing business with the poor. http://www.undp.org/gimlaunch. Accessed 16 May 2012
Zahra SA, Covin JG (1994) The financial implications of fit between competitive strategy and innovation types and sources. J High Technol Manag Res 2:183–211

Chapter 2
Corporate Social Entrepreneurship and New Business Models

Abstract The chapter analyzes social innovation at the level of the business model. The study clarifies the main characteristics and differences among alternative models of business to target the low income sector. Starting with the literature on social entrepreneurship and business models, a new theoretical framework "The Social Business Model Framework" is developed. The framework is used to identify the main characteristics of social business models and to emphasize the main area where social innovation can be applied.

Keywords Corporate social entrepreneurship • Business models • Social business • Inclusive business

2.1 The Emergence of Hybrid Enterprises

In the past decades, we have seen the emergence of two global phenomena. The first phenomenon is an evolution from the concept of Corporate Social Responsibility to the Creating Shared Value approach proposed by Porter and Kramer (2006). According to the authors, the capitalist system is sinking through a major crisis that is driving the need to revise the logic underlying the traditional business models; thus, "we need a more sophisticated form of capitalism, one imbued with a social purpose. But that purpose should arise not out of charity but out of a deeper understanding of competition and economic value creation. This next evolution in the capitalism model recognizes new and better ways to develop products, serve markets, and build productive enterprises" (p. 77).

The second phenomenon is the increasing role of emerging market economies (EMEs) in the global economy and the growing importance of the bottom of the pyramid market segment and, therefore, the beginning of the BOP 2.0 approach (see Table 2.1).

Both of these phenomena lead to a need for innovation and for the development of new business models. The borders between enterprises are becoming blurred, and companies are increasing their "area of action"; they will invade new space (for example, the public or the not-for-profit sector). Therefore, they are developing new ways of engaging with society; the area of competence

L. Michelini, *Social Innovation and New Business Models*, SpringerBriefs in Business,
DOI: 10.1007/978-3-642-32150-4_2, © The Author(s) 2012

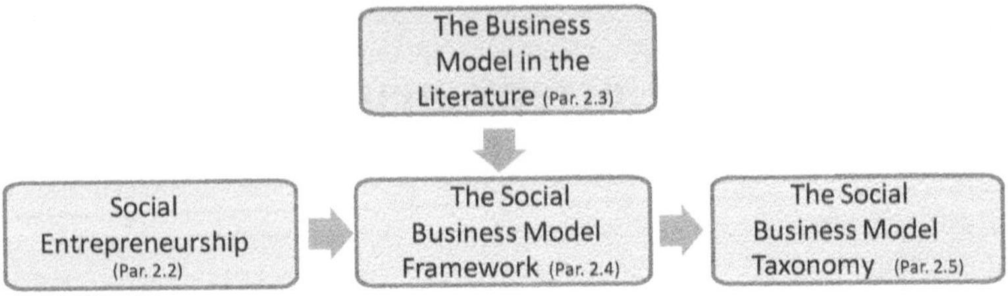

Fig. 2.1 The research process

includes simultaneously private (economic), public (political) and environmental (ecological) dimensions (Schieffer and Lessem 2009).

These new kinds of companies are defined as "integrated enterprises" or "hybrid enterprises", and they can generate different forms of social innovation. Hybrid enterprises are those enterprises "straddling the boundary between the for-profit business world and the social mission-driven public and not for profit organizations. Thus they do not fit completely in either sphere" (Hockerts 2006, p. 145).

Through these new enterprises, a new sector, called the "fourth sector", of organizations existing at the intersection of the public, private and social sectors is emerging (Fourth Sector Network 2009).

From this perspective, the aim of the following paragraphs is to identify the characteristics and distinct qualities of hybrid business models and to highlight where social innovation can be implemented to target the low-income market.

To reach this aim, first, the literature on social enterprises is analyzed to identify the main definitions and interpretations of the concept. Then, through an analysis of the business model literature, a new framework—the social business model framework—is developed. Finally, the framework is used to identify the main typologies of social enterprises and other forms of social innovations (Fig. 2.1).

2.2 Defining Social Entrepreneurship

In attempting to apply the principle of the creating shared value approach, which is characterized by the concept of generating mutual value, many companies have started to create alternative models of governance and strategies or management schemes, which can refer to the social entrepreneurship (SE) and corporate social entrepreneurship (CSE) field of study.

The concept of social entrepreneurship is a relatively new field of study; however, the literature is extending, and at times, the approaches and definitions conflict. A lack of agreement persists regarding the domain, boundaries, forms and definitions of social entrepreneurship (Peredo and McLean 2006). Social entrepreneurship is defined broadly in some cases and narrowly in others; thus, the literature has not yet achieved a consensus.

In the recent literature, many authors have collected and analyzed the key definitions of social entrepreneurship. For example, to highlight the complexity in giving a precise definition, Dacin et al. (2010) analyze 37 different definitions that emerged from 1991 to 2010, OECD (2010) analyzes 29 definitions in use from 2000 to 2010, and Swanson and Zhang (2010) summarized 14 theoretical constructs developed from 1998 to 2010.

The interpretation of social entrepreneurship ranges from a narrow perspective to a broader one (Perrini 2007). In this variety, there is an intermediate position favored by some authors and institutions (Yunus 2008; UNDP/EMES 2008).

A narrow interpretation of the phenomenon considers social entrepreneurship to be a not-for-profit initiative in search of alternative funding strategies or management schemes to create social value (Austin et al. 2003; Boschee 1998).

Box 2. Social Entrepreneur, Social Entrepreneurship, Social Enterprise and Corporate Social Entrepreneurship (CSE)

The concept of social entrepreneurship typically refers to a process or behavior, while the definition of a social entrepreneur focuses on the founder of the initiative.

Social entrepreneurs, specifically, are individuals who initiate activities that are focused on a social mission while behaving as true entrepreneurs through their dynamism, personal involvement and innovative practices (UNDP, EMES 2008).

The definition of a social enterprise refers to the tangible outcome of social entrepreneurship. Hence, when we talk about social entrepreneurship, we refer to the process that invests in private people who are oriented to pursue opportunity and are satisfying unmeet social needs.

If this same process is applied to the business sector, we should refer to it as corporate social entrepreneurship (CSE), (Austin and Reficco 2009).

Two other conceptual frameworks are the source and foundation for CSE: corporate entrepreneurship and social entrepreneurship (Austin and Reficco 2009). Covin and Miles (1999) have defined the former as "the presence of innovation with the objective of rejuvenating or redefining organizations, markets, or industries in order to create or sustain competitive superiority." Social entrepreneurship has been defined as a process involving the innovative use of resources to pursue opportunities to catalyze social change or address social needs (or both), (Mair and Marti 2006). From the synthesis of these two processes, a new model of business emerges: the CSE concept. The fundamental purpose of CSE is to accelerate companies' organizational transformations into more powerful generators of societal betterment. CSE is not another form of CSR but rather is a process for invigorating and advancing the development of CSR (Austin and Reficco 2009).

For UNDP and EMES, social enterprises may be defined as "private, autonomous, entrepreneurial organizations providing goods or services with an explicit aim to benefit the community. They are owned or managed by a group of citizens, and the material interest of capital investors is subject to limits. Social enterprises place a high value on their autonomy and on economic risk-taking related to ongoing socioeconomic activity. Social enterprises are either legally prohibited from distributing profits or are structured to exclude profit as the main goal" (UNDP/EMES 2008, p. 18).

A similar interpretation of social entrepreneurship is given by Yunus (2008; 2010). He defines the social business as a subset of social entrepreneurship that operates as an enterprise, selling products and services to customers. Unlike traditional enterprises, there are no dividends for the shareholders. Investors who decide to set up a social business enterprise can take back the amount of money that they invested, after which the surplus would not be distributed among the partners. Any surplus revenue would be reinvested to improve the quality of the product or service or toward scaling up the social business.

The purpose of Yunus' social entrepreneurship is not to eradicate or contrast with the traditional business model; he considers social business to be new, alternative way for entrepreneurship. He excludes the hypothesis of a social business model that admits dividends for shareholders because "profit-seeking companies with a strong CSR commitment try to make their pursuit of profit consistent with social considerations. However, their commitment to making a profit inevitably limits their contributions to social causes. (…) By contrast a social business is designed exclusively to deliver social value" (Yunus 2010, p. 11).

Furthermore, Yunus (2008) proposed a second typology of the social business model: a profit-making company that is owned by poor people. In this case, even if the business is profit oriented, it could be considered a social business because it is permitted to improve the social condition of low-income people.

Other contributions on SE agree with the broader definition: social enterprises are considered to be "organizations seeking business solutions to social problems" (Thompson and Doherty 2006). Several researchers, specifically, provide evidence that in SE the concept of the social mission is central. According to this vision, SE is a process that aims to

- address significant/alleviate social problems/needs (Light 2006; Mair and Marti 2006; Korosec and Berman 2006);
- catalyze social change (Mair and Marti 2006);
- alleviate the suffering of the target group (Martin and Osberg 2007);
- benefit society with an emphasis on marginalized people and the poor (Schwab Foundation 2011), and;
- create and distribute new social value (Peredo and McLean 2006; Perrini and Vurro 2006).

Thus, all of these definitions agree that social entrepreneurship is a means to alleviate social problems and improve well-being. Furthermore, the definitions focus on the potential beneficiaries of social entrepreneurship activities: generically, as "the community" and, specifically, as the "target group".

A broader definition of SE was also given recently by the European Commission (2011), which considers the social enterprise to be "an operator in the social economy whose main objective is to have a social impact rather than make a profit for their owners or shareholders. It operates by providing goods and services for the market in an entrepreneurial and innovative fashion and uses its profits primarily to achieve social objectives. It is managed in an open and responsible manner and, in particular, involves employees, consumers and stakeholders affected by its commercial activities" (p. 2). The European Commission uses the terms social enterprise and social business synonymously.

According to the EU definition, the main characteristic of social enterprises is their primary social and environmental aim, independently from their legal forms.

The European Commission uses the term "social business" to cover "businesses providing social services and/or goods and services to vulnerable persons (access to housing, health care, assistance for elderly or disabled persons, inclusion of vulnerable groups, child care, access to employment and training, dependency management, etc.); and/or businesses with a method of production of goods or services with a social objective (social and professional integration via access to employment for people disadvantaged in particular by insufficient qualifications or social or professional problems leading to exclusion and marginalization) but whose activity may be outside the realm of the provision of social goods or services" (European Commission 2011, p.3)

A broader interpretation of SE also allows for an innovative form of business that is becoming more widespread: the inclusive business model.

As discussed in Chap. 1, the Bottom of the Pyramid Theory proposed by Prahalad (2004) is based on the concept of "serving the poor profitably". Profitability in the low-income sector could be achieved only if companies change their traditional opinions about developing countries, by no longer considering them to be a territory to exploit but a market composed of producers and consumers with specific needs, which, in turn, could be satisfied through specific and innovative business models.

An analysis of the literature suggests that the inclusive business model, along with the social business model, represent the most accommodating business models with which to implement the BOP 2.0 approach that honors the characteristics previously highlighted (Michelini and Fiorentino 2012).

The relationship between the inclusive business model and social entrepreneurship has been emphasized by Marquez et al. (2010), through a case study conducted on 12 inclusive businesses. The authors conclude the study by stating that social enterprises are distinguished from traditional ones by two main features: the social value that is created and the level of stakeholder involvement. Creating shared value is a key point in the inclusive business model, in addition to the need to engage with stakeholders to succeed and obtain mutual business and social opportunities. Thus, the inclusive business model "is driving a convergence between traditional enterprise and social enterprise, with very different organizations behaving similarity" (Marquez et al. 2010, p. 322).

The inclusive business model can offer new opportunities to a company to conduct business responsibly and, at the same time, generate economic and social value.

Inclusive businesses are based on models with which to "include the poor on the demand side as clients and customers, and on the supply side as employees, producers and business owners at various points in the value chain. They build bridges between business and the poor for mutual benefit. The benefits from inclusive business models go beyond immediate profits and higher incomes. For business, they include driving innovations, building markets and strengthening supply chains. And for the poor, they include higher productivity, sustainable earnings and greater empowerment." (UNDP 2008, p. 2).

For the SNV and the World Business Council for Sustainable Development (2008), the inclusive business model is "one which seeks to contribute toward the alleviation of poverty by including lower-income communities within its value chain while not losing sight of the ultimate goal of business, which is to generate profits" (SNV/WBCSD 2008, p. 2).

The inclusive business model is characterized by the involvement of the low-income sector in the following three ways:

1. as customers, where the poor are the primary target of the business and companies make products and services available at an affordable price;
2. as suppliers, distributors or business partners, where the poor are involved in their value chain and companies contribute to job creation and knowledge sharing but target the average or high-income local population, traditional/global markets, and non-profit local or international organizations, and;
3. as customers and as suppliers, distributors or business partners, where the poor are both targets and actors involved in the company's value chain.

The main characteristics that differentiate inclusive business strategies from traditional ones are summarized below (see Table 2.1).

Economic growth is considered, in any case, to be the primary driver for the companies that develop inclusive businesses (International Finance Corporation 2010). However, this aim is pursued alongside the ethos of "create value for all" (*co-value creation*) with the awareness that by doing business with the low-income sector, firms create the potential for the growth of new business while they improve poor people's lives. Hence, this business model "can give people the confidence and strength to escape poverty using their own means (UNDP 2008, p. 23). Indeed, the inclusive business model is based on the concept of the "value constellation". This concept refers to the process of generating value within the company's own value chain as well as the value network of its suppliers and partners (Norman and Ramirez 1993). From this perspective, the main focus of the business is not the company itself but the value-creating system "within which different economic actors—suppliers, business partners, allies, and customers—work together to co-produce value. Their key strategic task is the reconfiguration of roles and relationship among this constellation of actors in order to mobilize

Table 2.1 Principles of the inclusive business model

The "Co-"Principles in the inclusive business model
CO-value creation
The company generates value within its own chain while generating value with its suppliers and partners.
CO-dependency and co-evolution
The company has a strong link with the eco-system. The relationship is based on a mutual dependence that leads to co-evolution.
CO-learning
Knowledge and technology transfer from the top of the pyramid to the bottom and from the bottom to the top.
CO-invention
Knowledge sharing and engaging with the poor leads to innovation
CO-existence of local and global
A company can target both the local and the global market.

the creation of value in new forms and by new players" (Norman and Ramirez 1993, p. 66).

The inclusive business model is also characterized by a strong link with the ecosystem, which is an economic community based on the interaction of different organizations that are directed to the production of goods and services. It is more than the extended value chain. The ecosystem includes the structural environment, the regulators, the supporting organizations and other actors, such as competitors and neighboring communities. The relationship between the company and the ecosystem is based on a mutual dependence (*co-dependence*), and the company should evolve together with the actors in the environment (*co-evolution*), (Marquez et al. 2010).

The inclusive business model is characterized by a combination and transfer of knowledge and technology from the top of the pyramid to the bottom and from the bottom to the top (*co-learning*). For example, co-learning can refer to training and technical assistance from the company to the local producers or to the possibility for the company to access local knowledge, expertise and ideas. Co-learning is linked with *Co-invention*. Knowledge sharing at the top of the pyramid, with the wisdom and expertise at the bottom, enables co-discovery of new opportunities to serve those at the BOP (London 2008; Whitney and Kelkar 2004).

The last principle concerns the connection of the local with the nonlocal (London 2008). Indeed, the target of inclusive business models can be any of the following: local and nonlocal low-income people, middle and high income people (local and nonlocal), and non-profit local and international organizations (Michelini and Fiorentino 2012). Therefore, a company can take locally-produced goods and sell them in nonlocal markets, including both wealthier in-country and international markets. Furthermore, "a BOP venture can take a locally produced good, such as honey, and sell this product to BOP markets in other (nonlocal) regions or countries" (London 2008, p. 19).

In considering these definitions, it is possible to conclude that the term social entrepreneurship is used to refer to the rapidly growing number of organizations that have created models for efficiently satisfying the basic human needs that the existing markets and institutions have failed to fulfill. Social entrepreneurship combines the resourcefulness of traditional entrepreneurship with a mission to change society and to increase well-being. Whereas corporate social entrepreneurship (CSE) is this same process developed by an existing traditional company, CSE represents an evolution and an advanced interpretation of CSR.

At this point in the study, it is useful to reaffirm the relationship between social entrepreneurship and social innovation.

As emphasized at the end of Chap. 1, social innovation is implied in these forms of business models: *social innovation is generated by the combination of business model components that set up an enterprise with the aim of improving community well-being and, at the same time, guarantees economic and financial sustainability.*

From this perspective, the main aims of the next sections are to (1) identify the business model components that are useful for analyzing social enterprise and (2) distinguish the boundaries and differences among social and inclusive businesses and the general concept of social entrepreneurship.

2.3 The Business Model in the Literature

The academic literature offers various definitions and perspectives of the concept of business models that can be useful for an analysis of the CSE models of inclusive and social businesses (Michelini and Fiorentino 2012).

The tool—the business model—was established with the aim of understanding the dynamics of technological change and was used to represent the processes of managing IT systems (Jones 1960; Konczal 1975). Thus, the purpose of the business model concept has been historically defined by emphasizing value creation as a part of managing the development of technology. It was considered to be "a coherent framework that takes technological characteristics and potentials as inputs and converts them through customers and markets into economic outputs. The business model is conceived as a focusing device that mediates between technology development and economic value creation" (Chesbrough and Rosenbloom 2002, p. 532).

Because of the emergence of the New Economy, the use of the business model has greatly increased. Researchers and managers had the need to define "new business formulas" and to identify models that could express the concept of value creation.

Indeed, the recent pressure to gain access to markets in developing countries, particularly those at the middle and bottom of the pyramid, is driving a surge in business-model innovation (Casadesus-Masanell and Ricart 2011).

However, Drucker in 1954 had already clarified the importance of a business model that can answer the following questions: Who is your customer? What does the customer value? How do you deliver value at an appropriate cost? Many

Table 2.2 Business model components in the literature

Authors	Business model components
Casadesus-Masanell and Ricart (2011)	Policy choices, asset choices, governance choices
Yunus et al. (2010)	Value proposition (stakeholders and product/service), social profit equation (social profit and environmental profit), value constellation (internal value chain and external value chain) and economic profit equation (sales revenues, cost structure, and capital employed)
Osterwalder et al. (2005) also used by Marquez et al. (2010)	Value proposition, distribution channel, relationship with customers, partner network and revenue model
Osterwalder and Pigneur (2010)	Customer segments, value propositions, channels, customer relations, revenue streams, key resources, key activities, key partnerships, cost structure
Zott and Amit (2010)	Design elements (content, structure, governance) and design themes (novelty, lock-in, complementarities, efficiency)
Rasmussen (2007)	Value proposition, market segment and revenue model, value chain, cost structure and profit potential, value network, competitive strategy
Hamel (2000) also used by Mair and Schoen (2005)	Core strategy, strategic resources, customer interface and value network

researchers define a business model by specifying its main components (see Table 2.2).

Zott and Amit (2010) define a business model as "the content, structure, and governance of transactions designed so as to create value through the exploitation of business opportunities" (2010, p. 219).

Recently, Casadesus-Masanell and Ricart (2011) maintain that a business model consists of "a set of managerial choices and the consequences of those choices" (p. 103), and the following are its main components:

- policy choices, which determine the actions an organization takes across all its operations;
- asset choices, which pertain to the tangible resources a company deploys, and;
- governance choices, which refer to how a company arranges rights decision making.

Osterwalder et al. (2005) suggest a definition that integrates two perspectives: the way a company conducts business and the conceptualization of the strategy. For the authors, a business model is "a conceptual tool containing a set of objects, concepts and their relationships with the objective to express the business logic of a specific firm. Therefore we must consider which concepts and relationships allow a simplified description and representation of what value is provided to customers, how this is done and with which financial consequences" (2005, p. 5).

Recently, Osterwalder and Pigneur (2010, p. 14) suggest that "a business model describes the rationale of how an organization creates, delivers, and captures value" and propose the following building blocks for designing business models:

- value proposition, which presents an overall view of a company's products and services;
- target customers, which include the segments of customers to whom a company wants to offer value;
- distribution channel, which describes the various means through which the company engages with its customers;
- relationship, which explains the type of links a company establishes between itself and its various customer segments;
- value configuration, which describes the arrangement of activities and resources available to the company;
- core competency, which outlines the competencies necessary to execute the company's business model;
- partner network, which portrays the network of cooperative agreements with other organizations that are necessary to efficiently offer and distribute value;
- cost structure, which sums up the monetary consequences of the company's means employed in the business model, and;
- revenue model, which describes the way a company makes money through a variety of revenue flows.

Recently, some authors have used the concept of business model to analyze new forms of business (e.g., social and inclusive business).

Mair and Schoen (2005) referred to Hamel's business model components—core strategy, strategic resources, customer interface and value network—to identify the common features and patterns across the business models of successful social entrepreneurship.

Marquez et al. (2010), with the main aim of analyzing the specificity of the inclusive business model, selected some building blocks identified by Osterwalder et al. (2005) for their study. Specifically, they used the following components: the value proposition, the distribution channel, the relationship with the customers, the partner network and the revenue model.

Yunus et al. (2010) identified four components of a social business model: the value proposition (the stakeholders and the product/service), the social profit equation (the social profit and the environmental profit), the value constellation (the internal value chain and the external value chain), and the economic profit equation (the sales revenues, the cost structure, and the capital employed).

Michelini and Fiorentino (2012) adapted Osterwalder's framework to identify the main difference between the social and inclusive business models. Specifically, the authors used the following categories and sub-categories for their analysis: the value proposition, the ecosystem (e.g., governance, the value chain, skills, and the network partners), the market (the customers and the distribution) and the economic features (revenue management).

2.4 The Social Business Model Framework

This literature review indicates that researchers, who have explored new forms of business using the business model concept, need to adjust the traditional business model frameworks. This need for adjustment is because the traditional frameworks have limitations in analyzing new forms of hybrid enterprises, in which the social component is of great importance.

In fact, the traditional models are not able to capture all of the specific aspects of these new forms of enterprise. Specifically, they do not allow for an analysis that highlights the specific features and innovations relating to the revenue management model, the model of governance and the social impact of the business.

In light of this shortcoming, a new framework was developed to define a model that could be used as tool for the analysis of new business forms and as a tool to analyze the creation of social innovation.

The model was developed from a literature analysis on business models and in consideration of the specificity of the new forms of business that were described above.

Specifically, the social business theoretical framework has developed, emerging from the frameworks of Osterwalder et al. (2005) and of Yunus et al. (2010).

The social business model framework is composed of the following 7 areas, which include 13 components:

- *offer*, which is characterized by the *value proposition* that is the benefit offered by the company through products and services;
- *market*, which includes the *market segment,* the segments of customers that a company wants to reach; the *relationship,* which describes the communication strategy and type of connection that the company establishes with its customers; and the *distribution*, which describes the various channels that a company uses to reach its customers;
- *governance*, which relates to the *governance model* of the company and includes the set of processes or laws that manage the relationship between stakeholders as well as the goals for which the corporation is governed;
- *ecosystem*, which includes the *value chain,* which refers to the chain of activities for a firm operating in a specific industry, and the *competences*, which outline the specific range of proficiency (skill, knowledge, or ability) of a company, and the *partner network*, which refers to the network of cooperative agreements with other organizations that are necessary to efficiently offer and distribute value;
- *surplus*, which describes how the company manages the revenue surplus. (Does it include dividends for shareholders?);
- *economic profit equation,* which includes the *costs structure* and *revenue model*, and;
- *social value equation*, which describes the way a company generates *social benefit* (in terms of risks and benefits) (Fig. 2.2).

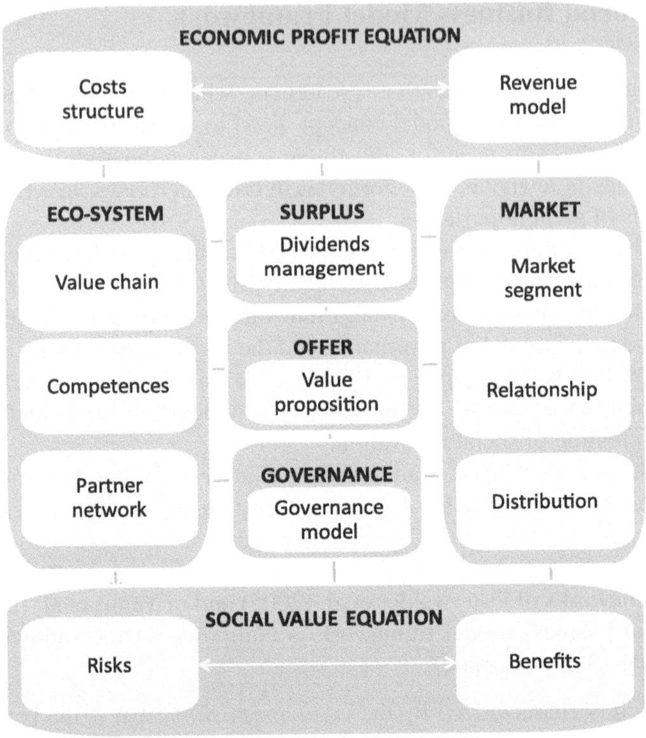

Fig. 2.2 The social business model framework

The components identified above will be used to highlight the main characteristics of the new forms of enterprise and to highlight the areas where social innovation can be expressed.

Specifically, we anticipate the following:

- the *social and economic value equation* and the *surplus* will be used to classify the main forms of social business models;
- the *eco-system* and the *governance* will aid in the identification of unconventional forms of innovations, and;
- the *offer* and the *market* will be explored in the next chapter through the social product innovation process and communication strategies.

2.5 CSE for the Low-Income Market

To better understand the characteristics and differences between the business models, a taxonomy will be developed that considers the social business model framework (described in the paragraph above) and the main classification that exists in the literature (Dacin et al. 2010; Yunus et al. 2010; Massetti 2008; WBCSD 2008).

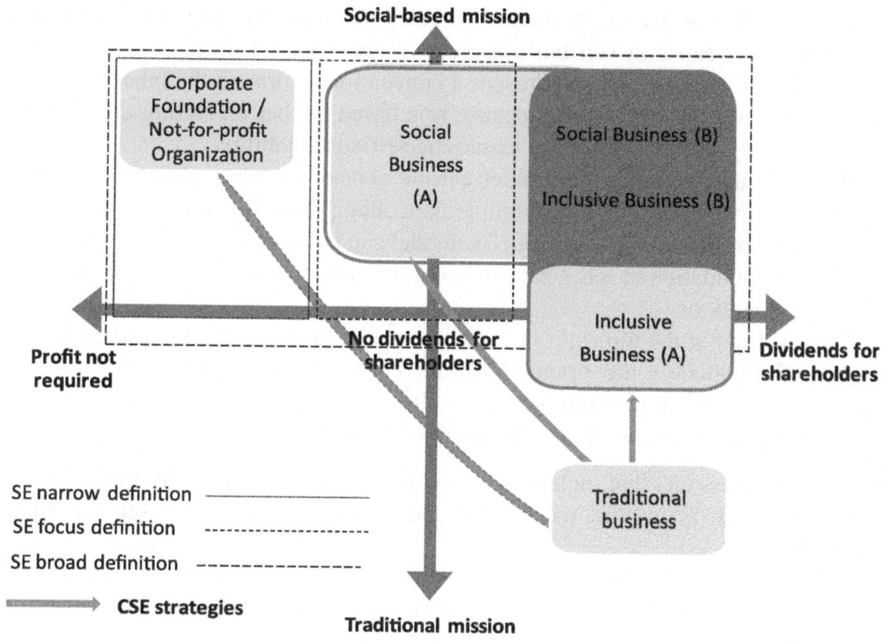

Fig. 2.3 The social business models taxonomy

From the literature review, two critical points emerge. The first point concerns the true meaning of the attribute "social" and how a social mission might distinguish SE from other organizational forms. The second point refers to the revenue model and surplus management as existing in a continuum from "profit not required" to "social business" and ending with "profit required".

In considering the components of the business model framework to develop the matrix, the following two variables have been selected:

- the *social* and *economic profit equation.* By comparing the economic and social value generated by the enterprise, it is possible to identify the social impact. The comparison identifies whether a company is more social or profit oriented (a market-based mission *versus* a social-based mission);
- the *surplus*. Surplus management can range from "zero surplus", where profits are not required, to profits are required and re-invested in the company (no dividends for shareholders), and to profits are redistributed among shareholders.

By using these two variables, a matrix can be developed wherein different forms of business models that target the low-income markets can be placed (Fig. 2.3).

The matrix identifies alternative CSE strategies that a traditional, existing company can implement to target low-income markets.

The traditional business model is located in the quadrant at the bottom right section of the matrix. This model is solely profit oriented, without consideration of social effects. The arrows show the alternative corporate social entrepreneurship strategies that a company can decide to pursue to target low-income markets.

The corporate philanthropy model, included in the area at the top left section of the matrix, is a cause-driven but not profit-oriented model. In reality, the philanthropic model itself does not represent a conventional form of the business model aimed at the low-income sector because it is based neither on selling a product or service directly to the poor nor on economic self-sustainability.

However, the philanthropic model can be considered a possible CSE strategy that the company can decide to implement along with the traditional business operation to increase the CSR level. The model can be accomplished by establishing a corporate foundation or a not-for-profit organization that is in charge of managing corporate donations.

The quadrant at the top right includes the social business and inclusive business models. Both models are oriented toward economic self-sustainability and are engaged in improving the community's well-being by generating profits.

The social business model is characterized by two mains typologies:

- social business (A) that includes the companies that do not distribute dividends; this approach is in line with the social business model proposed by Yunus (2008), and;
- social business (B) that includes all the companies whose mission is socially oriented independently from the financial management; this approach is in line with the European Commission's definition (2011).

The inclusive business model is a traditional business activities model that moves along the ordinate axis and depends on the social level of the mission (from A to B). The inclusive business model represents an intermediate model that appears between a traditional business focus on the CSR approach and a social entrepreneurship with a high social orientation. The position in the matrix depends on the strength and importance of the social mission in the balance of the social and profit equation.

Moreover, this matrix illustrates the relationships that exist among the three aforementioned areas. Essentially, a traditional company could choose to approach the low-income market by implementing inclusive or social business models.

Regarding the social business model, it may represent an evolution of the philanthropic models because their priority is not only to achieve social sustainability but also to reach their economic goals. Finally, depending on the firm's priorities (i.e., economic benefit *versus* social benefit), conversions between social and inclusive businesses models cannot be excluded.

2.6 Social Innovation in Governance and the Ecosystem

The matrix discussed above shows how the balance between the profit and social equation and surplus management can generate innovative forms of enterprise.

By using the remaining components of the social business model framework, it is possible to identify additional types of innovations that refer to the following components: the offer, the market, governance, and the ecosystem. The process and the innovation typologies concerning the offer and the market will be analyzed in the following chapter.

Social innovation can also refer to governance and the ecosystem areas.

These spheres of innovations relate to

- new forms of governance (governance innovation) and
- new forms of ecosystem relationships (relationship innovation).

Innovation in the governance system refers to the ability to identify new forms of control that allow for a balance between opposing or differing interests.

A traditional company that wants to enter in the low-income market—in line with the BOP 2.0 and the CSE approaches—has the following strategic options (Fiorentini 2006):

- build an internal spin-off company by forming a strategic social business unit (SSBU);
- modify the mission of the company by adding the social value, i.e., move from a market-based mission to a socially based mission, or;
- build an external spin-off company and decide which legal form to use (cooperatives, for-profit, non-profit) and how to manage the surplus (dividends or no dividends for shareholders).

New forms of governance can refer to the development of a profit-not-for-profit joint-venture (Yunus 2008). In this case, the partners establish a new legal entity called a social business enterprise (SBE). The governance model consists of the board of directors, which is made up of managers and professionals from the two founding organizations. Participation in the new entity in egalitarian ways helps to ensure that the specific interests of one of the two subjects could not prevail.

The second form of innovation refers to the eco-system. Concerning the eco-system, Marquez et al. (2010) affirmed that the most radical innovation that they observed—in their sample—was relational, which is a kind of innovation that is usually not found in traditional markets. This innovation comprised "ways of bringing together poor people and the company that wished to include them as a customers or suppliers and included the active participation of company personnel in low-income sector communal spaces" (p. 41).

The form of innovation that refers to the eco-system for the business model also relates to the market area (and the components of markets, relationships and distribution) and will be thoroughly analyzed in Chap. 4.

References

Amit R, Zott C (2001) Value creation in e-business. Strateg Manag J 6–7:493–520

Austin J, Reficco E (2009) Corporate social entrepreneurship. Working Paper n. 09–101, Harvard Business Schools, Boston

Austin J, Stevenson H, Wei-Skillern J (2003) Social entrepreneurship and commercial entrepreneurship: Same, different, or both? Working paper series no. 04–029 Harvard Business School

Boschee J (1998). Merging mission and money: A board member's guide to social entrepreneurship. http://www.socialent.org/pdfs/MergingMission.pdf. Accessed 15 May 2012
Casadesus-Masanell R, Ricart JE (2011) How to design a winning business model. Harvard Bus Rev 89(1):2–9
Chesbrough H, Rosenbloom RS (2002) The role of the business model in capturing value from innovation: evidence from Xerox corporation's technology spin-off companies. Indust Corp Change 3:529–555
Covin JG, Miles MP (1999) Corporate entrepreneurship and the pursuit of competitive advantage. Entrepreneurship Theory Pract J 3:47–63
Dacin P, Dacin M, Matear M (2010) Social entrepreneurship: why we don't need a new theory and how we move forward from here. Acad Manag Perspect 3:37–57
European Commission (2011) Social business initiative creating a favourable climate for social enterprises, key stakeholders in the social economy and innovation SEC(2011) 1278 final. http://ec.europa.eu/internal_market/social_business/docs/COM2011_682_en.pdf. Accessed 15 May 2012
Fiorentini G (2006) Impresa sociale e sussidiarietà. Franco Angeli, Milano
Fourth Sector Network (2009) The emerging fourth sector. http://www.fourthsector.net/learn/fourth-sector. Accessed 15 May 2012
Hamel G (2000) Leading the revolution. Harvard Business School Press, Boston
Hockerts K (2006) Entrepreneurial opportunity in social purpose ventures. In: Mair J, Robinson J, Hockerts K (eds) Social entrepreneurship. Palgrave Macmillan, Basingstoke
International Finance Corporation (2010) Scaling up inclusive business: advancing the knowledge and action agen http://businessinnovationfacility.org/forum/topics/inclusive-business-2010-ifcda. Accessed 16 May 2012
Jones GM (1960) Educators, electrons, and business models: a problem in synthesis. Account Rev 4:619–626
Konczal EF (1975) Models are for managers, not mathematicians. J Syst Manag 1:12–15
Korosec RL, Berman EM (2006) Municipal support for social entrepreneurship. Publ Adm Rev 66:448–462
Light PC (2006) Reshaping social entrepreneurship. Stanford Social Innovation Review
London T (2008) The base of the pyramid perspective: a new approach to poverty alleviation. In: Paper presented at the academy of management annual meeting. Academy of Management, Anaheim. pp. 1–46
Mair J, Marti J (2006) Social entrepreneurships research: a source of explanation, prediction and delight. J World Bus 1:36–44
Mair J, Schoen O (2005) Social entrepreneurial business models: an exploratory study. Working paper n. 610, IESE Business School, Madrid
Marquez P, Reficco E, Berger G (2010) Socially inclusive business: engaging the poor through market initiatives in iberoamerica David Rockefeller center for Latin American Studies. Harvard University Press, Cambridge
Martin RJ, Osberg S (2007). Social entrepreneurship: The case for a definition. Stanford social Innovation Review, Spring pp. 29–39
Massetti BL (2008) The social entrepreneurship matrix as a "Tipping Point" for economic change. E:CO 3:1–8
Michelini L, Fiorentino D (2012) New business models for creating shared value. Soc Responsib J 8 (Forthcoming)
Norman R, Ramirez R (1993) From value chain to value constellation: designing interactive strategy. Harvard Bus Rev 4:65–77
Organization for Economic Co-operation and Development (OECD) (2010). SMEs, Entrepreneurship and Innovation. http://www.oecd.org/document/16/0,3746,en_2649_33956792_44938128_1_1_1_1,00.html. Accessed 11 May 2012
Osterwalder A, Pigneur Y (2010) Business model generation. Wiley, Hoboken
Osterwalder A, Pigneur Y, Tucci CL (2005) Clarifying Business models: origins, present, and future of the concept. Commun Am Indian Stud 1:1–25

Peredo AM, McLean M (2006) Social entrepreneurship: a critical review of the concept. J World Bus 1:56–65
Perrini F (2007) Social entrepreneurship. Egea, Milano
Perrini F, Vurro C (2006) Social entrepreneurship: innovation and social change across theory and practice. In: Mair J, Robinson J, Hockerts K, London (Eds) Social entrepreneurship, Palgrave Macmillan, UK pp. 57–85
Porter ME, Kramer MR (2006) Strategy and Society. The link between competitive advantage and corporate social responsibility. Harvard Business Review, Boston pp. 78–92
Prahalad CK (2004) The fortune at the bottom of the pyramid: eradicating poverty with profits. Wharton Business Publishing, Philadelphia
Rasmussen B (2007) Business models and the theory of the firm. Working paper n. 32 CSES, Victoria University, Melbourne
Schieffer A, Lessem R (2009) Beyond social and private enterprise: towards the integrated enterprise. Trans Stud Rev 15:713–725
Schwab Foundation (2011) Social entrepreneur of the year India 2011, Social entrepreneurship for inclusive growth. http://www.jubilantbhartiafoundation.com/seoy-profile-booklet-2011.pdf. Accessed 16 May 2012
SNV and World Business Council for Sustainable Development (WBCSD) (2008) Inclusive business: profitable business for successful development. http://www.wbcsd.org/Pages/EDocument/EDocumentDetails.aspx? ID=13709&NoSearchContextKey=true. Accessed 16 May 2012
Swanson LA, Zhang DD (2010) The social entrepreneurship zone. J Nonprofit Public Sect Mark 2:71–88
Thompson J, Doherty B (2006) The diverse world of social enterprise: a collection of social enterprise stories. Int J Soc Econ 33(5/6):361–375
United Nations Development Programme (UNDP), European Research Network (EMES), (2008), Social enterprise: a new model for poverty reduction and employment generation. http://europeandcis.undp.org/ourwork/poverty/show/02F5569C-F203-1EE9-BD529F-7FE21C9320 Accessed 15 May 2012
Whitney P, Kelkar A (2004) Designing for the base of the pyramid. Des Manag Rev 4:41–47
World Business Council for Sustainable Development (WBCSD), SNV Netherlands development Organization (2008) Inclusive business: profitable business for successful development. http://www.wbcsd.org/includes/getTarget.asp?type=d& id = MzExNDQ. Accessed 14 May 2012
Yunus M (2008) A world without poverty: social business and the future of capitalism. Public Affairs, New York
Yunus M (2010) Building social business. Public Affairs, New York
Zott C, Amit R (2010) Business model design: an activity system perspective. Long Range Plan 2–3:216–226

Chapter 3
New Social Product Development: The Process and Critical Success Factors

Abstract In this chapter—through a literature review of the new product development process and innovation for low income markets—a new theoretical framework that describes the development process of social products is proposed. By using this social product development framework and a multiple-case studies analysis on best practices in social product innovation, this book presents factors that are critical to successfully developing social products for low-income markets. Finally, principles for the communication of social products are proposed.

Keywords Social product innovation • Low-income market • Critical success factors

3.1 Designing a Social Product for Low-Income Markets

Social innovation can also concern the component "offer" of the business model in terms of the *value proposition* that is the benefit offered by the company through products.[1]

A social product is a form of social innovation and, as a consequences, it should have the same features (described in Chap. 2). Therefore, social product innovation directed to the low-income sector should have the following features:

1. must generate a positive social impact;
2. is driven by both social and economic motivations;
3. must be novel;
4. can be promoted by different actors (businesses, NGOs, public institutions);
5. must be scalable;
6. must be sustainable;
7. can take different forms, and;
8. must improve and change the lives of the poor.

The literature sometimes uses the terms social and ethical products interchangeably. To define the characteristics of the social product and to highlight the

[1] The term "product" will be used in the sense of its broader meaning to refer to either tangible products or to services (or both).

DOI: 10.1007/978-3-642-32150-4_3,

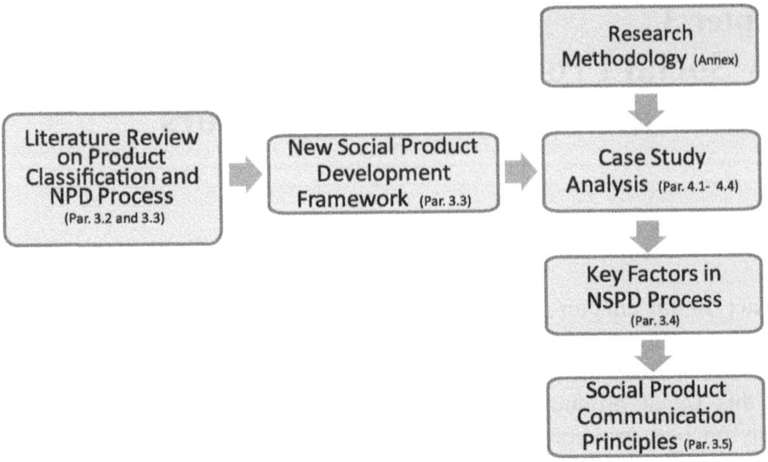

Fig. 3.1 Chapters 3 and 4: the process of the research

main differences from others' typologies (e.g., traditional and ethical products), it is important to better understand which are the characteristics that determine its being "social" or "ethical", specifically in the case of low-income markets.

To this end, starting from the analysis of the academic and managerial literature, a classification of products based on the social and ethical dimensions will be presented.

The literature on new product development (NPD) will then be analyzed, and by capturing the common phases of the process, a new framework is proposed that describes the social product development process.

By a multiple case study analysis of social innovation best practices (described in the Chap. 4), this chapter provides the critical factors that are necessary to develop successful social innovations with which to target the low-income market. Finally, principles for social products marketing communication are presented (Fig. 3.1).

3.2 The Literature on Product Classification

One of the first classifications of products that was based on an ethical dimension was developed by Kotler in (1972). He classified products along two dimensions: immediate satisfaction and long-run consumer welfare. The four resulting classes of products were (i) deficient products, which offered neither immediate satisfaction nor long-run consumer welfare (for example, smokeless cigarettes with an unpleasant smell and taste); (ii) pleasing products, which provided immediate satisfaction but had a detrimental impact on consumers in the long run (for example, sweets); (iii) salutary products, which were worthy in the long run but were less attractive in regard to immediate satisfaction (for example, washable diapers); and (iv) desirable products, which offered the advantageous combination of having high levels of immediate satisfaction and high levels of long-run consumer welfare (for example, fairly traded bananas).

In the traditional market, the use of the ethical and social attributes has been considered a source of differentiation. Categories of attributes are considered to be an element that adds value to existing products or services and, to increase interest, form a specific niche in the market and enhance the perception of the company's social responsibility.

The consumer's social and environmental consciousness obliges the producers to seek out cultural differentiation for their products, and it is a process that may specifically include ethical conduct or at least respect for the consumer's primary rights. Such rights include information, health and safety, promised quality, freedom of choice, and the desire of the purchaser to be listened to and be treated on the basis of parity (Giaretta 2005).

Levitt (1980) contends that the product can be conceptualized at the following three different levels: the core product, which is the fundamental benefit, or solution to a problem, sought by the consumers; the expected (or actual) product, which is the basic physical product that delivers those benefits and; the augmented product, which is the addition of extra or unsolicited services or benefits to the consumer to prompt the purchase. Starting from Levitt's notion of the augmented product concept, Crane (2001) asserts that the content of ethical augmentation can, therefore, refer to the following levels:

- products: ethical augmentation can be viewed in terms of those issues that are directly related to the actual product or service;
- marketing: even at the marketing level, augmentation can be positively directed (e.g., a cause-related marketing campaign) as well as negatively directed (the campaigns can misrepresent the product);
- corporations: the level relates not to the specific product nor even to its marketing but to the firm general behaviour that actually supplies the product, and;
- countries: the most indirect level of product augmentation that can be identified is in terms of the country with which the product or its manufacturer might be associated. For some consumers, their purchases' country of origin is a significant ethical consideration.

Beginning from the Crane framework and considering the product level, it is possible to make the following classification (Michelini 2006):

- *non ethical products*, which are those products that are damaging in terms of abuse (e.g., alcohol) or inherently damaging (e.g., tobacco), socially controversial, environmentally incompatible, and which fail to guarantee the consumers' security;
- *intrinsically ethical products*, which are products that respect ethical criteria that is compatible with the environment or the consumers' security and which,

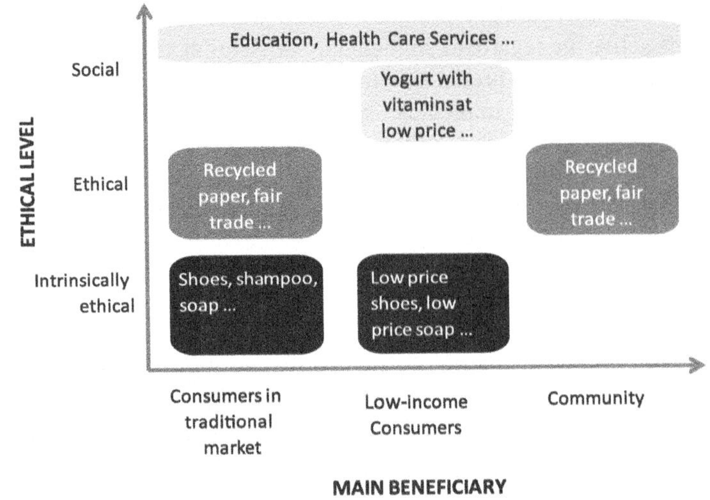

Fig. 3.2 Products taxonomy on ethical level and main beneficiary

according to Giaretta's definition (2000) "generate a positive impact, or in the least don't induce damaging effects";

- *ethical (or sustainable) products*, which are products that are different than the inherently ethical products, in that they have an added ethical attribute beyond the actual product that the company chooses to communicate to the consumer. The ethical product is unique because (1) it is connected to a specific ethical problem, (2) it puts the consumer in the position of having to choose between an ethical and a non-ethical product, and, (3) it reflects a personal, rather than a business, decision to act in an ethical fashion in the production of a determined good. The client that acquires the ethical product is aware that the purchase contributes to a specific cause. For example, the consumer is aware that in purchasing an ecologically friendly detergent, he or she is contributing to an effort to avoid damaging the environment, and in purchasing impartial or jointly liable products, the consumer can help sustain a developing country, and;
- *socially useful products*, which are those products that can have two main features based on the object and on the target. The first typology refers to the social aim of the product: for example, medical services or education. The second typology refers to the target and includes all products developed specifically for a disadvantaged category of people (for example, the people at the bottom of the pyramid or the disabled, seniors or persons suffering illness) and presents specific added value (with respect to the intrinsically ethical products) that allows for an increase in well-being (e.g., yogurt with vitamins).

In the Fig. 3.2, a taxonomy of products is shown that considers two variables: the ethical level (from intrinsically ethical to social, excluding non ethical product) and the main beneficiary of the product (consumers in traditional markets, low-income consumers and the community).

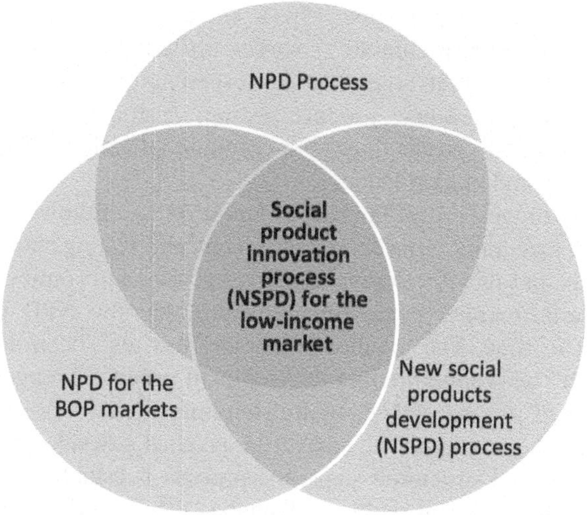

Fig. 3.3 The field of studies on product innovation

3.3 The Process of New Social Product Development

The process of new product development (NPD) involves activities and decisions that begin with the generation of an idea (from various sources) and continue until the product's commercialization, e.g., it is launched into the market (Craig and Hart 1992).

To develop a framework for the development of social products for the low-income segment, it is useful to summarize the main academic literature on this topic. Specifically, these studies can be classified into three main fields (see Fig. 3.3):

- studies on new product development (NPD) process;
- studies on new product development (NPD) for the BOP market;
- studies of new social products development process.

There is extensive literature on the new product development process. Studies show two main models of NPD process activities: linear (or sequential) activity and parallel (or interactive) activity.

The linear model in NPD process is proposed by several authors. The linear model has two possible configurations that are determined by identifying the primary influence for innovation. Thus, innovation can be characterized as being influenced by:

- a technology push, if the innovation is driven by the opportunities offered by technological development, or;
- a market pull, if the innovation is driven by market needs.

Among the studies on linear models of innovation, Cooper and Kleinschmidt (1986) analyze the NPD process of 203 products. The authors have used a framework of the process that is based on various studies developed by other researchers

(Little 1970; Utterback 1971; Cooper 1983). The model includes the following 13 phases: initial screening, preliminary market assessment, preliminary technical assessment, detailed market study/market research, business/financial analysis, product development, in-house product testing, customer product testing, test market/trial sell, trial production, pre-commercialization business analysis, production start-up and market launch.

Kotler (1980) suggests a NPD process based on the following 8 major steps: idea generation, screening, concept development and testing, marketing strategy, business analysis, product development, market testing and commercialization.

In other words, parallel processing indicates that the NPD phases are performed parallel in time. The parallel processing has also been defined also as a "rugby approach" where the product development process emerges from the constant interaction of a hand-picked, multidisciplinary team whose members work together from the beginning to the end of the product's development. Rather than moving in defined and structured steps, the process is established from the interplay of the team members Takeuchi and Nonaka (1986). In the literature review on the NPD process, Craig and Hart (1992) conclude that there is a theoretical section of the literature that suggests that a simultaneous, rather than sequential, approach to developing new products is more successful. Clark and Fujimoto (1991) consider product innovation to be a rehearsal of future customers' product experiences. The authors claim that effective product development rests on the ability of a product's design to create a positive product experience, and they emphasize the importance of managing the product's information from the customers to the production of the product, to sales and back to the customers. Thus, the innovation process is divided into the following three parts: the product development process (characterized by three sources of input—the market, the strategic plan and technological sources), the production process and the consumption process.

Pratesi and Mattia (2002) propose an NPD framework that considers an overlap of some of the phases during the process. The process starts with the generation of the idea and the validation, the targeting and positioning, and then there is the phase of test marketing that is linked to (and in context with) the marketing mix planning and the financial and economic evaluation. The process ends with the product launch.

Michelini (2006) proposes a specific model of the product innovation process that is based on a consumer-ethic driven approach. This theoretical framework describes the innovation process that allows companies to improve the ethical characteristics of the product. The first phase (a products and social problems analysis) includes an evaluation of the ethical implications connected with the current company's products and an analysis of the main social problems to be solved. In the second stage (the generation of the idea), the ideas should be developed and new products should emerge from technological opportunities or from a market needs analysis. The company's next task is to select the concepts, developing those ideas that are considered more interesting (through financial and economic evaluation). The process ends with the definition of a marketing mix strategy and the launch of the product(s).

The emerging BOP literature has recently focused on product innovation processes that, when targeting the base of the pyramid, presents unique product development challenges as well as new opportunities.

In terms of product development opportunities, the literature suggests some important factors (Prahalad 2009; Donaldson 2006; Viswanathan and Sridharan 2011):

- people ask not only for affordable products but also for high quality and value-added products;
- there are new opportunities for multifunctional product design, and;
- success in BOP markets depends on the ability to be consistent with local conditions and to develop user-centric products that involve local skills.

According to Prahalad, product innovation should focus on the 4 As (2006, 2011):

- creating awareness, such that the consumers and producers at the bottom of the pyramid know what products and services are available;
- enabling access, such that even those consumers in remote areas are able to gain access to the products and services;
- developing affordability, such that the products and services are affordable, and;
- focusing on availability, such that there is an uninterrupted supply of products and services that are provided by the company.

Prahalad (2006, 2011) describes the importance of going beyond the traditional approach of the product innovation process and facing the new difficulties of emerging and developing countries. According to the Prahalad Innovation Sandbox theory, a company should start identifying the core constraints that they must overcome to obtain a breakthrough innovation. These constraints are limitations that force unconventional thinking in several directions (that are, for example, specialization or pricing). Thus, a company can develop a sandbox that allows it to identify the constraints, and within those limits, it can strengthen its creativity. Moreover, Prahalad suggests two main important criteria to adopt in product development:

- innovation must start with a deep immersion into the customers' lives to gain unique insight, which allows the company to identify the constraints within which the company can innovate, and;
- innovation is about developing an ecosystem, which is an integral part of innovation.

In addition, Chandra and Neelankavil (2008) highlight the need to rethink the process of new product development in developing countries. According to the authors, unlike the traditional NPD process, the social product innovation process should start from a view of limitations or constraints. Therefore, the new product development process for developing countries should start with two basic questions: "at 'what price point' would the low-income population be able to afford a product/service?" and "what is the 'value-added' element to the customers in using the new product (in other words, does the new product solve some customer problems)?" (p. 1022).

One of the most focused articles on the product development process for the BOP was written by Viswanathan and Sridharan (2011). In the article, the authors identify 11 key factors that are necessary for a successful product development for BOP markets (when compared with the non-BOP markets). These factors refer to the following:

- identification of the critical basic needs of consumers;
- identification of the consumers' hopes and goals;
- an emphasis on envisioning situations for the product's use;
- an emphasis on serving multiple purposes;
- an emphasis on customization at the point of purchase;
- an emphasis on customization for low-literate users;
- an emphasis on local sustainability;
- an emphasis on leapfrogging the lack of infrastructure;
- an emphasis on leveraging the existing infrastructure where available;
- an emphasis on incorporating the product-related infrastructure, and;
- an emphasis on adding on to existing products.

Because of the growth of new products that have the aim of creating social value, in recent years, some authors have also began to analyze the topic of the product development process in the field of social innovation. Although the theme of social innovation is very well developed and highly topical, the academic literature on the subject remains sparse thus far.

One of the more exhaustive articles specifically on the process of social innovation is by Mulgan (2006), who identifies four main phases of the process. The starting point is obtaining ideas, understanding needs and identifying potential solutions. The second stage is developing, prototyping and piloting the ideas. The third phase of the social innovation process begins when the idea has been tested and can grow, replicate and diffuse. Finally, the fourth stage is focused on learning and evolving; "innovation continues to change, and learning and adaptation turn the ideas into forms that may be very different from the expectations of pioneers" (Mulgan 2006, p.154).

Recently, the European Union (2012) claims that research on the social innovation process tends to converge on a homogeneous view of the following main phases of the process: (1) ideas, (2) prototype and piloting, (3) implementation and (4) scaling.

An interpretation of the process according to the traditional linear approach—characterized by a market pull or a technology push approach (Fig. 3.4(1)—leads to evidence of a new linear model of social innovation for the low-income sector. The model starts with limitations that influence the research, the development and finally the production of new products (Fig. 3.4(2). However, if we look at the evolution of this marketing approach for the low-income sector, it is clear that this approach is linked with the BOP 1.0 model, where new products were primarily adapted to the local market (generally in terms of low costs). Innovation was constraints-driven and that primarily indicated that there was low-cost-driven innovation.

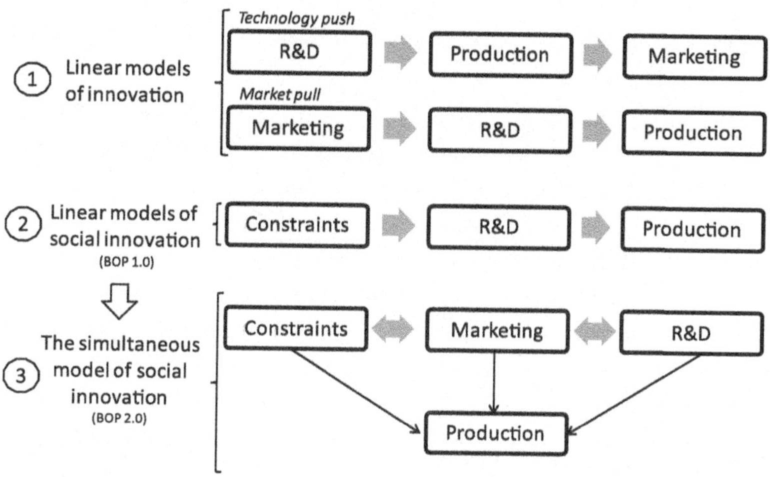

Fig. 3.4 Models of innovation

The evolution from BOP 1.0 to BOP 2.0 models also has an effect on the new product development process. Companies that decide to target the low-income market with social products should consider simultaneously the importance of identifying constraints; analyzing consumers' needs and taking advantage from technology (Fig. 3.4(3)).

3.4 New Social Product Development Framework

The previous literature review has shown that numerous frameworks for the new product development process have been developed. Although each contribution has its own peculiarity, they have some common elements regarding the main phases of the process. Starting from the literature analysis on NPD and capturing the common phases, a new framework that describes the social product development process to target the low-income market is proposed (Fig. 3.5).

Specifically, the proposed framework is an adaptation of the model proposed by Pratesi and Mattia (2002) and by Michelini (2006), regarding the specific nature of the social product for the low-income market. The framework was built considering the limits of the linear approach and the problem related to the overlap of some of the phases in the product development process.

The new social product development (NSPD) process is characterized by six main phases. The first phase is idea generation includes three main approaches:

- market driven, if the development of the new concept starts form customers' needs;
- technology driven, if the new product is derived from technological inputs, or;
- constraints driven, if the source of creativity is the restrictions and limits of the ecosystem.

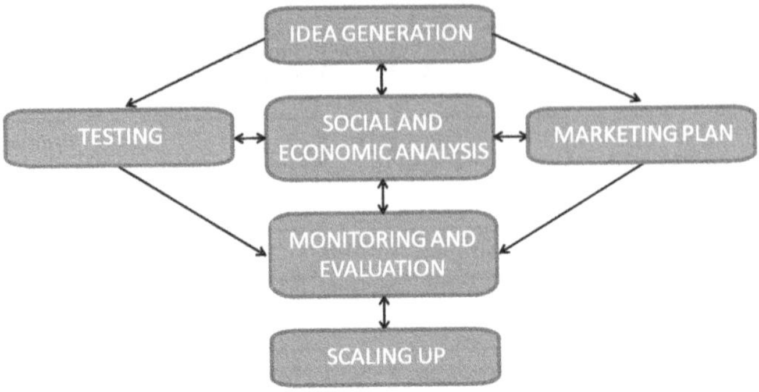

Fig. 3.5 New social product development framework

The testing phase is concerned with the laboratory tests and the field studies.

The marketing plan phase includes the definition of the marketing strategy (the marketing objectives, the targeting and positioning) and the development of the social marketing mix (the product, the price, the distribution, the promotion and the packaging).

Unlike a traditional NPD model, the NSPD framework includes the social and economic equation analysis. This phase is concerned with the economic and financial analysis of the investment and considers both the economic benefits for the company and the social effects of the project on the society and on the local community. This phase is simultaneous with the marketing plan phase.

This step is at the center of the framework because can be developed at each phase of the process from the beginning with idea generation to the final phases of evaluation and scaling up.

The monitoring and evaluation phase refers to the audit of economic and social outcomes of the project.

Finally, the scaling up phase can be considered an optional and additional step. In this phase, the company might consider the possibility of a quantitative (e.g., extending the geographic area of distribution) or functional (e.g., product differentiation) scaling up.

By using the theoretical framework for NSPD, a multiple-case study analysis of the best practices in social product innovations was developed. Specifically, the following case studies were analyzed:

- PuR, developed by Procter and Gamble (P&G), is a product capable of purifying water at the household level, which is useful in reducing illness in children;
- Plumpy'nut, developed by Nutriset, is a ready-to-use product for the treatment of severe acute malnutrition;
- Shokti Doi, developed by Grameen Danone, is a yogurt that is fortified with calcium, proteins and micronutrients, which are essential elements children's growth, and;
- Interceptor, developed by BASF, is an insecticide-treated mosquito net that aims to reduce insect-borne diseases, such as, malaria.

For a detailed description of each case study see Chap. 4. For further information on the methodology used in this study, see Appendix: Research Methodology.

3.5 Key Success Factors in Social Product Innovation

The case study analysis has contributed to the identification of key success factors in the social product innovation process. The analysis leaves out considerations about different forms of business models and focus solely on the innovation process whereby social products directly target (as in the case of Shokti Doi and PuR) or indirectly target (as in the case of Plumpy'nut and Interceptor) the low-income sector.

First, there are three key factors that must be considered throughout the entire process (idea generation, testing, social and economic analysis, the marketing plan, monitoring and evaluation, and scaling up).

The first concerns the *importance of creating a specific team of work that is characterized by specific knowledge as well as research and decisional autonomy.*

In fact, from the analysis of the Procter and Gamble case history emerges an account of the usage of skunk works[2] methodology to support the research and development of new social products. The creation of a dedicated group is evident also in the case of Nutriset, which has established two specific divisions within the R&D department: the External Research and Nutritional Strategies Division (RESN) whose aim is to develop nutritional solutions to meet the specific needs of vulnerable communities around the globe and the Internal Research and Development Division (RDI) that is responsible for product development.

The literature identifies two main critical factors that contribute to the development of successful new products: (1) the involvement of top management (Ramanjam and Mensch 1985) and (2) cross-functional cooperation (Maidique and Zirger 1984; Pinto and Pinto 1990). The case studies confirm these proposals. In fact, it is important to underline that in all cases, the research team consisted of people from various departments in the company as well as from various organizations that jointly cooperated on the research project.

In conclusion, the analysis of the case studies has shown also that *the creation of dedicated intercompany research teams* represents a critical element for thriving in the field of social product innovation.

---

[2] A skunk works is a small group of people who work on a project in an unconventional way. The group's aim is to develop something quickly with minimal management constraints. Skunk works are often used to initially develop a product or service that thereafter will be developed according to usual business processes. Recently, many companies have created skunk works to solve the problems of inflexibility, slow innovation, and avoidance of change, where innovation could thrive unimpeded by bureaucracy (Ghoshal and Bartlett 1995). The term skun kworks was first introduced during World War II by engineers at Lockheed (Source: http://www.lockheedmartin.com).

Table 3.1 Company's partners along the social innovation product process

Phases	Partners
Idea generation	Research institutes, public health players and humanitarian organizations
Testing	Research institutes, consumers, Public health players and humanitarian organizations
Social and economic analysis	Public players and humanitarian organizations
Marketing plan	Public players, local community and humanitarian organizations
Monitoring and scaling up	Humanitarian organizations, local community, local enterprise, public players
Scaling up	Local community, local enterprise, public players

The third factor is *the importance of partnering with external stakeholders* to succeed in new social product innovation. This importance has been already been shown since the first phase of idea generation. The partnership between research institutes, universities, humanitarian organizations, and public health players represents a fundamental aspect of the social innovation process (Rondinelli and London 2003; Hart and Sharma 2004). In the PuR case as well as in the Plumpy'nut innovation process, the cooperation between the company with non-traditional stakeholders characterizes all phases of the product's development.

Considering the four case histories, Table 3.1 summarizes which stakeholders were involved in each phase of the product's social innovation process. Specifically, these case studies have shown that during the idea generation phase, it is extremely useful for companies to cooperate with the research institute, public health players and humanitarian organizations. This cooperation allows companies to better understand the unmet needs of the low-income segment and to understand the requirements for effective social solutions.

A business will reap greater benefits from engaging in a sustainable livelihoods business model if it is able to transfer the lessons it has learned and its successes to other areas of operation or to efforts to enter new markets. Partnering with a local SME or with organizations (e.g., a government or no-profit organization) whose mission is to strengthen small and medium businesses can help to achieve this objective.Even if cooperation with external organizations for the research and development of new products is not often discussed in the traditional managerial literature (Kuczmarski 2003), there is some evidence of this new trend. Gupta, Pawar and Smart (2007) assert that in the pharmaceutical/biotech landscape, the new industry dynamics, which are largely driven by technological change, are shifting the locus of knowledge and value creation away from the firm and toward a network of firms.

The Economist (2010) highlights that, today, companies and new stakeholder groups increasingly see a future in collaboration rather than in confrontation. However, differences among groups remain, and they are particularly differences regarding working culture and goals. "Thus companies must be prepared to work closely with these groups on some initiatives, while facing attacks by those same groups over perceived abuses in other areas of operations" (p. 4).

UNDP and WEF have both documented the importance of collaboration for gaining access to assets, capabilities, and knowledge and for sharing costs and risks (UNDP 2008; World Economic Forum 2009).

Previously, Polosky et al. (1998) have analyzed the importance of cooperating with "non-traditional" stakeholders in developing green products. They assert that the greening process requires that firms include other non-traditional groups, for example, environmental special interest groups. Within the green NPD process, learning from, understanding and "managing" non-traditional stakeholder interactions is extremely important.

In analyzing inclusive business case studies, WBCSD (2008) suggest that one major element in every successful corporate effort to generate a sustainable livelihoods business is a strategy of partnering with external resources whether it be with the expertise of a development organization or with the complementary skills of another corporation.

The development of a partner network along with the development of the social innovation process could be also defined as a "*business friendship*". This term refers to the need for building a close, personalized and sustained relationship that extends well beyond a "one-shot" commercial value exchange to operate in the market (Marquez et al. 2010). The term is related to the concept of "business intimacy" (Simanis and Hart 2008) that is built when companies and the community view each other interdependently, developing a mutual commitment to each other's long-term growth.

The term "business friendship" refers to a relational dynamic with a long term scope that extends beyond the market transaction. Customer value proposition in the low-income segment entails more than adding to a product or service. Companies tend to focus on innovations that deliver a product for the "job-to-be-done". While this is required and sustainable, innovations that go beyond the "job-to-be-done" are best suited to make an impact on society and to be inclusive (CII-ITC CESD 2010).

Figure 3.6 summarizes the main findings that emerged from the analysis of the case studies for each phase of the social product innovation process.

3.5.1 Idea Generation

Concerning the idea generation phase, the four cases indicate the need *to investigate and understand local and specific problems through a deep understanding of the local community, starting from the constraints and restrictions they must overcome or wish to overcome.* Thus, building a deep dialogue with the community is mandatory to better understand local needs.

This finding is consistent with what has been stated by Simanis and Hart (2008) and Prahalad (2006, 2011). Simanis and Hart (2008) in emphasizing the concept of building deep dialogue with the community, also explain methods that might include cohabitation to establish trusting relationships with families and to

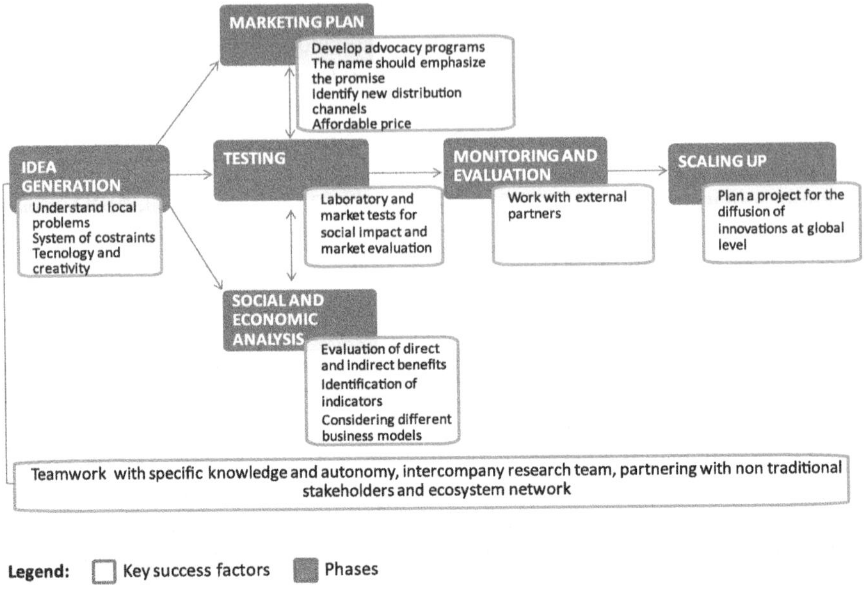

Fig. 3.6 Key success factors in social product innovation

empathize with their needs. Following the families, the corporate team lives in the community, if possible, to maximize informal relationship-building opportunities and to reinforce the corporation's commitment to working with the community. Prahalad (2006, 2011) use the concept "Innovation sandbox", which is a tool that can be used to identify the core constraints that companies must overcome to achieve a breakthrough innovation.

This perspective, emerging from the literature review on product innovation for targeting the base of the pyramid, is more evident when the company is planning to develop a social product. For example, P&G initially developed NutriStar, which was design for a developing-world problem but was created with a developed world mindset. Rather than being designed for a low price, it included the latest technology. P&G also found that it had insufficient in-country infrastructure to deliver its product "down-market", or to the poorest communities. In summary, they did not consider the local constraints.

As Viswanathan and Sridharan (2011) also suggest, an effective concept and prototype development for the BOP should place the emphasis on leapfrogging because of the lack of infrastructure. In some cases, for example, companies operated in conditions that lacked power or road infrastructure.

The second finding, which in part derives from the previous one, refers to the need to combine the following four factors for the development of the concept and the prototype: *the identification of social problems, the identification and evaluation of internal and external constraints, the identification of technology opportunities, and the use of creativity* (Fig. 3.7).

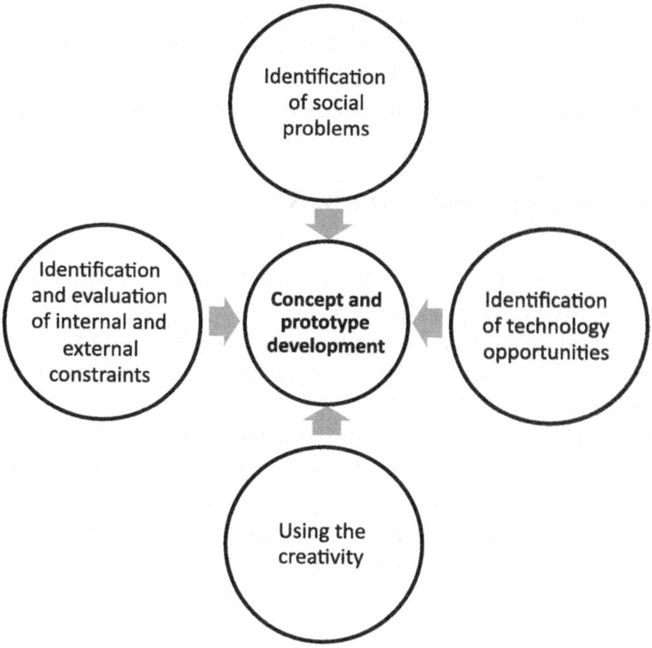

Fig. 3.7 Concept and prototype development

3.5.2 Testing

In the testing phase, the effectiveness of the product is experienced through tests in laboratories as well as in the field.

The field test can be conducted to identify which features of the product to improve (e.g., flavor), to identify any possible resistances to consumption, and to evaluate the marketing plan decisions (e.g., the price and the packaging).

In this phase, it is extremely important to have the support of the partners who are specifically in not-for-profit organizations and the partners who are public health players, who both help companies individuate and engage the target group. Once a company has achieved a better understanding of the real needs of its markets, it is ready to develop the product market plan. To succeed, it must be based on a customer-oriented approach that often requires lateral thinking about providing integrated solutions rather than isolated products to holistically address their needs. Engaging directly with communities as well as local governments or humanitarian agencies helps to define the right marketing mix to promote the offer.

Finally, laboratory tests are required to evaluate the safety and the efficacy of the product.

In conclusion, the testing phase in the social product development process is not so different from a traditional testing phase. However, the case studies analysis allows for the consideration of two specific factors. First, the *laboratory and field test must be developed to evaluate both the product's efficiency in solving the social problem and to evaluate the marketing mix decisions.* Second, the *involvement of the external partners* is fundamentally to guarantee the success of the testing phase because they can help the company involve the target group.

3.5.3 Social and Economic Analysis

Starting from the testing phase, the company must evaluate the social and economic feasibility of the entire project.

Unlike a traditional product, *a social product needs an evaluation of the social effects and of the direct and indirect benefits by the identification of qualitative and quantitative indicators.*

For example, Danone's social analysis includes an evaluation of the following indicators: employment growth (for example, in terms, of the number of Danone employees, the number of jobs created in the rural area), local entrepreneurial development (for example, in terms of the number of farmers involved in the Danone value chain, the number of new local enterprises), and nutritional status (for example, as measured throughout the children's growth cycle in terms of height, the cognitive performance of children and their capacity to concentrate and learn).

From an economic point of view, case studies show the importance of *considering different business models,* such as:

- commercial models, where the product is sold direct to the final customers (e.g., Danone);
- social models, which involve the not-for-profit organizations or public institutions in the distribution process (e.g., BAF), and;
- a combination of commercial and social models (e.g., P&G).

3.5.4 Marketing Plan

The case studies show the importance of develop *advocacy programs aimed at local communities.* In fact, case studies emphasize the important role that communication plays in building demand at the community level. Moreover, to carry out a successful educational campaign for the community, specific communication skills are required. In the PuR case study, the main challenge for P&G was to promote a change in consumer habits. From this point of view, it is clear that educational efforts, including product demonstrations, are necessary to encourage a change in consumer habits.

Moreover, all case studies suggest that *the name of the product should emphasize its promise.* This emerges from the four case studies analyzed here: Shokti Doi means Yogurt for Power, PuR is an abbreviation of Purify, Interceptor highlights the ability to block out mosquitoes, and the name Plumpy'nut refers to the concept of a nutritive food that is ready to eat.

Another key point in this phase is the importance of *identifying alternative distribution channels* to respond to the territory's characteristics and to local demands. For example, Danone has a unique door-to-door distribution system. Danone developed a door-to-door sales strategy that is ensured by the "Grameen Ladies". These women are trained to deliver a nutritional message (that underlines the importance of combining sales with advocacy programs), and they receive a commission for each yogurt that they sell.

Finally, all case studies show the importance of *establishing an affordable price while guaranteeing additional benefits for the customer*. This task requires not cutting costs in product development but creating new products with a value add at a lower price. Defining the right offer requires an understanding of the low-income market and the ability to identify additional benefits to satisfy specific needs while maintaining a low price level.

3.5.5 Monitoring and Evaluation

Measuring and reporting on the benefits generated for the company and for the community is essential for efficient communication, but it is also essential for improving or fine-tuning the company's activities.

A measure of the benefits to communities can not being achieved without the support of a local partner and humanitarian organization, which are able to verify the relationship between trends in social problem and the diffusion and use of social products.

In this phase, more than in others, it is necessary to *work with external partners* (for example, not-for-profit organizations or public institutions). An external partner can

- provide the company with the expertise and knowledge needed for measuring the social effects and to collect and analyze data;
- provide data and indicators concerning the social context (e.g., the death rate, the level of malnutrition, the education rate), and;
- guarantee reliability of the data output. A third party report or a joint report can be a guarantee of data impartiality and reliability.

For example, International Medical Corp and World Vision were involved in the distribution of PuR in a specific country, and at the end of the project, they have developed a detailed report with complete information concerning the results and social effects of the product.

3.5.6 Scaling Up

All case studies highlight the importance of ***planning a project for the diffusion of innovation at a global level***. This process is called a "scaling up", which refers to the increase in the scope of an activity, program, project, or initiative so that it serves more people or delivers more or better benefits (WRI 2008).

Since Plumpy'nut was first developed in 1996, the possibility of producing the product locally has been central to the principle of nutritional autonomy upheld by Nutriset. Following the initially small-scale trials (in Mauritania, Burkina Faso, Niger, Malawi and Sudan), Nutriset formalized this technology-sharing approach in 2005 by creating the Plumpy'nut in the field network, since renamed PlumpyField.

P&G, on the basis of its filtration technologies and knowledge, developed a new product line that is used in water purification, which they sell in traditional markets (e.g., PuR MineralClear, PuR ClassicClear).

The academic also literature highlights the fact that successful innovations need to move beyond the pilot phase to scale-up according to a pre-determined business model (Mulgan 2006; Christensen et al. 2006; WWF and CII-ITC CESD 2008).

The World Resources Institute (WRI 2008) has stated that there are five forms of scaling-up: quantitative (size expanding, increasing profitability and/or repetition in new geographic areas), functional (repetition in type or content of inclusive activity), organizational (increasing the replicability of skills and processes for other initiatives), political (a strengthening of a firm's contractual power to obtain more political support), and institutional (the growth and the improvement of institutions that are necessary to the ecosystem).

3.6 Social Product Communication Principles

The final objective of a social innovation marketing plan is the diffusion of the social innovation. Diffusion is defined as the process by which an innovation is adopted and its gains are acceptance by members of a specific community (Surry 1997). A number of factors interact to influence the diffusion of an innovation. Rogers (1995), in describing his Innovation Decision Process theory, recognizes the following influencing elements: the innovation itself, how information about the innovation is communicated, and the time and the nature of the social system into which the innovation is being introduced. Starting from these assumptions, Rogers states that the diffusion is a process that occurs over time and that can be considered to have five distinct stages: knowledge, persuasion, decision, implementation and confirmation.

According to Rogers' theory, potential adopters of an innovation must learn about the innovation, be persuaded as to the merits of the innovation, decide to adopt it, implement the innovation, and confirm (or reaffirm or reject) the decision to adopt the innovation.

Having clarified the diffusion of a social innovation, its characteristics and its steps, it is now necessary to understand how it should be implemented; in other words, how are social innovators able to diffuse their innovations? The social marketing literature gives useful answers to this question. On the basis of Rogers' theory (1995), it is possible to affirm that the diffusion and the acceptance of a social innovation is connected to sociological, anthropological and communication factors. Alternatively, social marketing—like generic marketing—is a framework or structure that draws from many bodies of knowledge, such as psychology, sociology, anthropology and communications theory to understand how to influence people's behavior (Kotler and Zaltman 1971). Hence, a strong link is evident between the diffusion of a social innovation and the social marketing framework.

The term "social marketing" was coined by Philip Kotler and Gerald Zaltman in (1971). This term refers to the application of principles and techniques drawn from the commercial sector to influence a target audience to voluntarily accept, reject, modify, or abandon a behavior for the benefit of individuals, groups, organizations, or society as a whole. The intent of social marketing is to create positive social change. This idea dates back to 1951, when Wiebe challenged the marketing community by asking "Why can't you sell brotherhood and rational thinking like you sell soap?" (Wiebe 1951/1952) and caused people to begin to think seriously that methods that were successfully used to influence behavior in the commercial sector might transfer to the non-profit arena. Social marketing can be applied to promote merit products and services, or it can be applied to induce a target audience to avoid demerit products and services, thus promoting its well-being (Serrat 2010).

Andreasen (1995) describes social marketing as the application of commercial marketing technologies to the analysis, planning, execution and evaluation of programs designed to influence the voluntary behavior of target audiences to improve their personal welfare and that of society (p. 7). This definition reveals social marketing's four key features. The first is a focus on changing voluntary behavior: social marketing is not concerned with coercion or enforcement. Second, social marketers try to induce change by applying the principle of exchange—the recognition that there must be a clear benefit for the customer if change is to occur (Houston and Gassenheimer 1987). Third, marketing techniques, such as consumer oriented market research, segmentation and targeting, and the marketing mix should be employed. Finally, the end goal of social marketing is to improve individual welfare and society, not to benefit the organization performing the social marketing tasks; this end goal is what distinguishes social marketing from other forms of marketing (MacFadyen et al. 2002).

The primary aim of "social marketing" is "social good", while in "commercial marketing", the aim is "financial" (Mahesh 2007). If the basic objective of corporate marketers is to satisfy shareholders, the bottom line for social marketers is to meet society's desire to improve quality of life. Meeting this desire requires a long-term approach to planning that moves beyond the individual end user to groups, organizations, and society, (Serrat 2010). Consumer marketing might aim to influence the brand choice of an individual (e.g., a brand of toothpaste), while social marketing aims to influence the behavior of the individual in relation to oral hygiene (e.g., increase the frequency of teeth cleaning), (Kotler & Andreasen 1987).

It is also important not to confuse "social marketing" with other types of "commercial marketing" that contribute to a social good but that do not have the primary aim to contribute to a social good. Kotler and Lee (2004) distinguish corporate social initiatives in six macro-categories: corporate social marketing; cause promotion (sometimes called "cause marketing," supporting social causes through paid sponsorships or promotions); cause-related marketing (donating a percentage of revenue from the sale of specific items during an announced period of support); corporate philanthropy (including direct cash grants to a charity or cause); community volunteering (wherein employees are encouraged to volunteer in the local community); and socially responsible business practices (discretionary activities, such as the use of recycled and reduced packaging, which is intended to align a corporation's conduct with a generally perceived social good). Corporate social marketing is different from all other social initiatives categories because in these cases the "social good" is not the primary goal, but only a related goal to support the companies' commercial and financial aims. In social marketing, the distinguishing feature is therefore its "primary" focus on "social good", and thus, this good is not a secondary outcome.

The emphasis on society as well as the individual also illustrates another key point concerning social marketing: it can apply not only to the behavior of individuals but also to that of professionals, organizations and policymakers (Stead et al. 2007). Social marketing can be applied downstream as well as "upstream". It might seek to change the behavior of professionals, the behavior of retailers (making them more compliant with the law for selling tobacco or alcohol to minors or persuading them to refrain from stocking confectionery in the checkout area), and the behavior of policymakers and legislators (convincing them to pass smoke free legislation, improve housing policy, or restrict advertising aimed at children) (Hastings et al. 2000; Lawther et al. 1997).

In conclusion, social marketing could be defined as a long term process oriented to the "social good" that has changed the behavior of an entire community at the downstream level as well as at the upstream one. A central principle in the social marketing mindset is a commitment to understanding consumer behavior to identify individual and social barriers that could provide an obstacle for social innovation. Those applying social marketing methods need to know the people whose behavior they want to change—their aspirations and values, their relevant beliefs and attitudes, and their current behavioral patterns. Social marketers also look at the broader social and cultural factors that influence consumer behavior, recognizing that behavioral change is influenced by a combination of environmental as well as personal and interpersonal factors.

Most initiatives to foster sustainable behavior rely on large-scale information campaigns that utilize education and/or advertising to encourage changes in behavior. While education and advertising can be effective in creating public awareness and in changing attitudes, numerous studies show that changes in behavior rarely occur as a result of merely providing information. Community-based social marketing is an attractive alternative to information-based campaigns (McKenzie-Mohr and Smith 1999).

Community-based social marketing is sourced in research in the social sciences that demonstrates that changes in behavior are most effectively achieved through initiatives delivered at the community level that focus on removing barriers to an activity while simultaneously enhancing the benefits of the activity.

The single most important step in designing an effective program for change is choosing specific, action-oriented, realistic and achievable behavioral objectives. It is vital to ask how feasible is a desired behavior likely to be from the point of view of the specific audience? (Robinson and Glanznig 2003).

To make people accept change, they must perceive their real needs and identify their real problems. In the UK, the National Social Marketing Center (2012) recognizes a strategic importance to the scoping stage—it drives the entire process. At the scoping stage, the primary concern is to establish clear, actionable, and measurable behavioral goals to ensure focused development throughout the rest of the process. In this phase, an assessment of consumer needs should be initiated to answer the following questions: What the audience should know/would like to know? What does the audience actually know? What is the GAP?

The PRECEDE to the module, developed by Green and Kreuter (1991), suggests that individuals need to be considered in the context of their community and society as a whole, when social marketing strategies are developed. Individuals are influenced by,

- predisposing factors, such as knowledge, attitudes, behavior, beliefs, and values prior to intervention that affect their willingness to change;
- enabling factors, such as the structure of the environment or community and the individual's situation that facilitate or present obstacles to change, and;
- reinforcing factors, such as the positive or negative effects of adopting the behavior that influence continuing the behavior.

In 2002, Andreasen identified six essential benchmarks of a "genuine" social marketing intervention:

- behavior change: intervention seeks to change behavior and has specific measurable behavioral objectives;
- consumer research: intervention is based on an understanding of consumer experiences, values and needs;
- segmentation and targeting: different segmentation variables are considered when selecting the intervention target group. Intervention strategy is tailored for the selected segment/s;
- marketing mix: intervention considers the best strategic application of the "marketing mix". The Four P's of marketing, i.e., Product, Price, Place and Promotion, are relevant in the case of social marketing. Four more P's can be added: Partnership, Policy, Politics and Participation by the audience;
- exchange: intervention considers what will motivate people to engage voluntarily with the intervention and offers them something beneficial in return. The offered benefit may be intangible (e.g., personal satisfaction) or tangible (e.g., rewards for participating in the program and making behavioral changes), and;
- competition: competing forces to the behavior change are analyzed. Intervention considers the appeal of competing behaviors (including current behavior) and uses strategies that seek to remove or minimize this competition.

Robinsons (2007), describing his seven doors models, states that rationalizations, confidence and convenience are behavioral factors that help changes to occur.

First, people need a grab-bag of beliefs and arguments with which they justify the change to themselves and others. Second, people need to believe they are capable of initiating a change and having the skills to follow it through to completion. Finally, it is a basic principle that new actions should be easy to accomplish, simple to understand and accessible.

Social marketing in developing countries is a new challenge for companies that decide to target the low-income markets. Unfortunately, in the few last years, a multitude of companies were involved in scandals and accused of instituting aggressive marketing policies in developing countries. What has been considered to be morally questionable was the aggressive misleading of potential customers though communications that neither reflected the framing conditions nor considered the actual knowledge standard for the consumer. The main critics in the field of marketing refer to price policies, bribery, unfair selling methods, unsafe products and deceptive advertising (Smith 1993).

These critics are fostering leading companies to increase a sense of responsibility in their marketing mix program.

As discussed in Sect. 1.4, social innovation can refer to the way in which an idea, a product or a service can be spread. The diffusion is the process by which an innovation is adopted and gains acceptance by members of a specific community Therefore, social innovation can identify new ways and tools of communication that are at the same time ethical and efficient in targeting the low-income market.In conclusion, a list of principles and approaches for responsible communication practices for both social and traditional products diffusion throughout low-income markets has been derived from literature and the case studies analysis.

In planning and define tools and contents of communication—both for traditional and social products—a company should do the following:

- *take into account the customer capability of judgment*. In fact, the ability of be analytic and critic depends on the cultural level and on market participation, and it is still evolving in developing countries. Especially "with regard to the impact of mass communication, it is necessary that companies consider the knowledge situation of the consumers as well as their cultural background when planning and defining the content of their communication measures" (Sele 2006, p. 100);
- *increase consumer's ability to evaluate and make comparison among products*. In fact, "although marketing thought recognizes that purchasing decisions are influenced by all sorts of impulses, the greatest ideal remains that of a rational consumer. Thus, buyers should be educated so that they make informed choices" (Witkowski 2005, p. 19);
- *consider the cultural background*, so an advertising campaign should be adapt to the local context, instead of the global context. The main aim should be to preserve a national and local identity, rather than promote an international one. Companies should be aware of the cultural identities of local consumers and accept it. These conditions can facilitate the creation of more informed customers (Sele 2006; Witkowski 2005);

- *plan advocacy and educational campaigns.* Along with a traditional communication, it is important to develop an advocacy and information campaign. Specifically, the main objective of the campaign should be (1) to educate to the correct use of the product and to avoid incorrect use or abuse and (2) to stimulate a correct behavioral link with the product's features (e.g., a soap's communication campaign of should explain the importance of hand washing before eating) (Michelini and Fiorentino 2012). In the academic field of development studies, advocacy campaigns are considered a prior condition to promote innovative solutions for improving health in the local community. In fact, a local commitment is essential to ensure that a community is invested in the success of a social innovation (Mulgan 2006);
- *use alternative and unconventional communication tools.* It is important also to consider that there are many ways that villagers can get new information: demonstration projects, street fairs, theater, radio broadcasts, pamphlets, posters, and video presentations can all broadcast possibilities, shift perceptions, and change tastes, making people more aware of options for action (Lobo 2007). It is also important use simple education materials in local languages, use images or strip cartoon, and include product demonstrations to encourage a consumer habit change;
- *rethink packaging design.* Considering packaging as one of the communications tools, some remarks are necessary. First, the distribution infrastructures in developing and emerging countries are sometime in poor condition, so packaging must be more resistant to guarantee product conservation. Moreover, companies should be more societal oriented by focusing on special-needs customers (Vernuccio et al. 2010), for example, by adopting sachet packaging or single-serve packets (Prahalad and Lieberthal 2003), and;
- *improve product naming.* The product's name should be easy to understand and to repeat, and especially for social products, it should emphasize the value-add of the product.

References

Andreasen AR (1995) Marketing social change: changing behavior to promote health, social development and the environment. Jossey-Bass, San Francisco

Andreasen AR (2002) Marketing Social Marketing in the Social Change Marketplace. J Public Policy Mark 1:3–13

Chandra M, Neelankavil JP (2008) Product development and innovation for developing countries. J Manag Dev 10:1017–1025

Christensen CM, Baumann H, Ruggles R, Sadtler TM (2006) Disruptive innovation for social change. Harv Bus Rev 84(12):94–101

CII-ITC CESD (2008). Indian companies with solutions that the world Needs. Sustainability as a driver for profit and innovation Impress, India http://www.sustainabledevelopment.in/publications/downloads/sustainability_driver_innovation.pdf. Accessed 11 May 2012

CII-ITC CESD (2010). Sustainable and inclusive innovation strategies for Tomorrow's world, cross media solutions. http://www.sustainabledevelopment.in/publications/downloads/SUSTAINABLE_INCLUSIVE_INNOVATION_24nov.pdf. Accessed 11 May 2012

Clark KB, Fujimoto T (1991) Product Development Performance. Harvard Business School Press, Boston
Cooper RG (1983) The new product process: an empirically based classification scheme. R&D Management 1:1–13
Cooper RG, Kleinschmidt EJ (1986) An investigation into the new product process: steps, deficiencies and impact. J Prod Innov Manage 3:71–85
Craig A, Hart S (1992) Where to now in new product development research. Eur J Mark 11:2–49
Crane A (2001) Unpacking ethical product. J Bus Ethic 4:361–373
Donaldson K (2006) Product design in less industrialized economies: constraints and opportunities in Kenya. Res Eng 3:135–155
European Union (2012) Financing social impact. Funding social innovation in Europe–mapping the way forward. http://ec.europa.eu/enterprise/newsroom/cf/_getdocument.cfm?doc_id=7048. Accessed 15 May 2012
Ghoshal S, Bartlett C (1995) Building the Entrepreneurial Corporation: new organizational processes, new managerial tasks. European Management Journal 6:139–155
Giaretta E (2005) Ethical product innovation: in praise of slowness. TQM Mag 2:161–181
Green L, Kreuter M (1991) Health promotion and planning: an educational and environmental approach (I2nd edn) Mayfield Publisher, Mountain View
Gupta A, Pawar K, Smart P (2007) New product development in the pharmaceutical and telecommunication industries: a comparative study. Int J Prod Econ 1:41–60
Hart SL, Sharma S (2004) Engaging fringe stakeholders for competitive imagination. Acad Manage Exec 18(1): 7–18
Hastings GB, MacFadyen L, Anderson S (2000) Whose behaviour is it anyway? The broader potential of social marketing. Soc Mark Q 2:46–58
Houston FS, Gassenheimer JB (1987) Marketing and Exchange. J Mark 4:3–18
Kotler P (1972) What consumerism means for marketers. Harvard Bus Rev 3:48–57
Kotler P (1980) Principle of Marketing. Prentice-Hall, Englewood Cliffs
Kotler P, Andreasen AR (1987) Strategic marketing for nonprofit organizations, Prentice-Hall (3rd edn), Englewood Cliffs
Kotler P, Lee N (2004). When it comes to gaining a market edge while supporting a social cause, 'corporate social marketing' leads the pack. Stanf Soc Innov Rev Spring 14-23
Kotler P, Zaltman G (1971) Social marketing: an approach to planned social change. J Mark 35:3–12
Kuczmarski TD (2003) What is innovation? And why aren't companies doing more of it? J Consumer Mark 6:536–541
Lawther S, Hastings GB, Lowry R (1997) De-marketing: putting Kotler and Levy's ideas into practice. J Mark Manag 4:315–325
Levitt T (1980) Marketing success through differentiation: of anything. Harv Bus Rev 58(1):83–91
Little B (1970) Characterizing the new product for better evaluation and planning. Working paper n. 21, University of Western Ontario, Canada
Lobo C (2007) Managing Trustee. Watershed Organisation Trust, Personal communication, May and July, Ahmednagar, Maharashtra, India
MacFadyen L, Stead M, Hastings GB (2002) Social marketing. In: Baker MJ (ed) The marketing book. Butterworth-Heineman, Oxford
Mahesh P (2007). Social marketing: a communication tool for development. In: Proceeding of international marketing conference on marketing and society, IIMK, India, 8–10(April)
Maidique MA, Zirger BJ (1984) A study of success and failure in product innovation: the case of the U.S electronic industry. IEEE Trans Eng Manage 4:192–203
Marquez P, Reficco E, Berger G (2010) Socially inclusive business: engaging the poor through market initiatives in Iberoamerica. David Rockefeller Center for Latin American Studies Harvard University Press, Cambridge
McKenzie-Mohr D, Smith W (1999) Fostering sustainable behavior: an introduction to community-based social marketing. New Society, Gabriola Island

Michelini L (2006) La dimensione etica nell'innovazione di prodotto. Economia, Impresa e Mercati Finanziari 1:89–111
Michelini L, Fiorentino D (2012) New business models for creating shared value. Soc Resp J 8 (Forthcoming)
Mulgan G (2006) The process of social innovation. Innovations: technology Governance. Globalization 2:145–162
National Social Marketing Center (2012) Social marketing tool, poadcast, http:// socialmarketing-toolbox.com. Accessed 14 May 2012
Pinto MB, Pinto JK (1990) Project team communication and cross- functional cooperation in new program development. J Prod Innov Manage 7:200–212
Polonsky MJ, Rosenberger PJ III, Ottman J (1998) Developing green products: learning from stakeholders. Asian Pac J Mark Logist 1:22–44
Prahalad CK (2006) The innovation sandbox. Strategy +. Business 44:1–10
Prahalad CK (2009) The fortune at the bottom of the pyramid: Eradicating poverty through profits, 5th edn. Wharton School Publishing, Upper Saddle River
Prahalad CK (2011) Bottom of the pyramid as a source of breakthrough innovations. J Prod Innov Manage 1:6–12
Prahalad CK, Lieberthal K (2003) The end of corporate imperialism. Reprinted in Harvard Business Review August 109–117
Pratesi CA, Mattia G (2002) Piano marketing dei nuovi prodotti. McGraw-Hill, Milano
Ramanjam V, Mensch GO (1985) Improving the strategy-innovation link. J Prod Innov Manage 4:213–223
Robinson L, Glanznig A (2003) Enabling EcoAction: a handbook for anyone working with the public on conservation. Humane Society International, WWF Australia, World Conservation Union, Sydney
Robinsons L (2007) The 7 Doors model for designing and evaluating behaviour change programs. The social Change Media. http://www.media.socialchange.net.au/strategy/7_Doors_Model.html. Accessed 14 May 2012
Rogers E M (1995) Diffusion of innovations (4th edn), The Free Press, New York
Rondinelli D, London T (2003) How corporations and environmental groups collaborate: Assessing crosssector collaborations and alliances. Acad Manag Executive 1:61–76
Sele K (2006) Marketing ethics in emerging markets: coping with ethical dilemmas. IIMB Manag Rev 18(1):95–104
Serrat O (2010) The future of social marketing. Knowl Solut 73:1–10
Simanis E, Hart S (2008) The base of the pyramid protocol: toward next generation BoP strategy. http://www.stuartlhart.com/sites/stuartlhart.com/files/BoPProtocol2ndEdition2008_0.pdf. Accessed 11 May 2012
Smith NC (1993) Ethics and the marketing manager. In: Smith and Quelch (Eds.), Ethics in marketing, Burr Ridge, Irwin pp. 3-34
Stead M, Gordon R, Angus K, McDermott L (2007) A systematic review of social marketing effectiveness. Emerald Health Educ 2:126–191
Surry DW (1997) Diffusion theory and instructional technology. In: Proceedings of the annual conference of the association for educational communications and technology (University of Southern Mississippi): Albuquerque, New Mexico pp.12–15
Takeuchi H, Nonaka I (1986) The new product development game. Harv Bus Rev 64(January–February) 137–146
The Economist Intelligence Unit Limited (2010) Dangerous liaisons. http://www.verizonbusiness.com/resources/reports/rp_dangerous-liaisons-eiu_en_a4_xg.pdf. Accessed 15 May 2012
United Nations Development Programme (UNDP) (2008) Creating value for all: strategies for doing business with the poor. http://www.undp.org/gimlaunch. Accessed 16 May 2012
Utterback JM (1971) The process of technological innovation within the firm. Acad Manag 14(1) (March):75–88
Vernuccio M, Cozzolino A, Michelini L (2010) An exploratory study of marketing, logistics, and ethics in packaging innovation. Eur J Innov Manag 3:333–354

Viswanathan M, Sridharan S (2011) Product development for the bop: insights on concept and prototype development from university-based student projects in India. J Prod Innov Manage 1:52–69

Wiebe GD (1951-52) Merchandising commodities and citizenship on television. Public Opin Q 15:679-691

Witkowski TH (2005) Antiglobal challenges to marketing in developing countries: exploring the ideological divide. J Pub Policy Mark 1:7–23

World Business Council for Sustainable Development (WBCSD), SNV Netherlands development organization (2008) Inclusive business: profitable business for successful development. http://www.wbcsd.org/includes/getTarget.asp?type=d& id = MzExNDQ. Accessed 14 May 2012

World Economic Forum (2009). The next billions: unleashing business potential in untapped markets WEF, Geneva, CH, http://www3.weforum.org/docs/WEF_FB_UntappedMarkets_Report_2009.pdf. Accessed 15 May 2012

World Resources Institute (WRI) in collaboration with united nations development programme, united nations environment programme, and World Bank (2008) World Resources 2008: Roots of Resilience—Growing the Wealth of the Poor. Washington, DC:WRI, http://pdf.wri.org/world_resources_2008_roots_of_resilience_front.pdf. Accessed 15 May 2012

Chapter 4
Case Studies Analysis

Abstract The chapter presents a description of four case studies on the social product innovation process: PuR, developed by Procter and Gamble, is a product able to purify water at the household level that useful for reducing illness in children; Plumpy'nut, developed by Nutriset, is a ready-to-use product for the treatment of severely acute malnutrition; Shokti Doi, developed by Grameen Danone, is a yogurt fortified with calcium, proteins and micronutrients, which are essential elements for children's growth; Interceptor, developed by BASF, is an insecticide-treated mosquito net that aims to reduce insect-borne diseases, such as malaria.

Keywords Social product innovation • Case studies analysis

4.1 PuR by Procter & Gamble

4.1.1 Overview

Established in 1837, The Procter & Gamble Company (P&G) began as a small, family operated soap and candle company in Cincinnati, Ohio, USA. Today, P&G markets almost 300 products to more than five billion consumers in 140 countries.

In 1999, Procter & Gamble (P&G) had made a strategic commitment to sustainable development. In particular it had articulated its vision that it was looking for opportunities to use its technologies to develop products and services that improve the lives of consumers in both developed and developing countries. A special role in this field has been played by the P&G Health Sciences Institute which has been charged to look for solutions useful to satisfy consumer needs in poor countries.

In 2003, the Procter & Gamble Health Sciences Institute, in collaboration with the International Council of Nurses (ICN) and the US Centers for Disease Control and Prevention (CDC), announced the launch of PuR, a new product able to provide clean drinking water for people in the developing world.

Today P&G has ten Global & Advocacy Partners, e.g., World Health Organization (WHO) and the U.S. Agency for International Development (USAID) and about 30 local Partners working on the front lines (e.g., World Vision and Save the Children).

L. Michelini, *Social Innovation and New Business Models*, SpringerBriefs in Business, DOI: 10.1007/978-3-642-32150-4_4,

4.1.2 Idea Generation

The first tentative to address the unmet needs was made through the launch of a product called NutriStar, a low-cost, powdered drink mix that contained all the vital micro-nutrients and also tasted good.

Despite the goodness of the product, the results achieved were disappointing, but provided an important learning experience. In particular the weaknesses of NutriStar were related to its pricing and its distribution. In fact NutriStar was design for a developing world problem, but with a developed world mindset. It included all of the latest technology, rather than being designed for a low price. P&G also found that it had insufficient in-country infrastructure to deliver its product 'down-market', or into the poorest communities.

Some year later, starting from the statements that more than 1 billion people do not have access to safe water and that the lack of safe water remain a leading cause of illness and death in the developing world, with about two million children dying every year due to these diseases, P&G has worked in partnership with the International Council of Nurses (ICN) and the Centers for Disease Control and Prevention (CDC) to find alternative, affordable solutions to the problem of safe drinking water.

In developing countries it is possible to achieve safe drink water only through water pump which however are quite rare. A complementary approach to providing piped-treated water is through treatment of drinking water directly in people's homes.

The aim of P&G research was to find a product able to purify water at the household level. Starting from this issue the PuR product has been created. The PuR product uses the same ingredients as those in municipal water systems, but is reverse engineered to effectively be a mini-water treatment plant in a sachet. A 4-gram packet of PuR treats 10 liters of water. PuR effectively kills bacteria and viruses and removes parasites and solid materials.

4.1.3 Testing

PuR has been tested in two ways: in laboratory tests for removal of pathogenic bacteria, viruses, and parasites as well as a selection of heavy metals and organics and on the field in five countries (Guatemala, Kenya, Pakistan, Philippines and South Africa) for removal of turbidity and fecal organisms. The Centers for Disease Control and Prevention have conducted two large health intervention trials to determine effectiveness in reducing diarrheal disease. The testing studies show that use of PuR can reduce diarrheal illness in children by an average of 50 %.

4.1.4 Marketing Plan

PuR was created by building on past SL business experience. Learning from the NutriStar experience, PuR has been designed for a price point that is realistic for the target populations. One small sachet, costing about US$ 0.10 in the commercial model, will treat 10 liters of water (enough drinking water for an average family for 2 days).

The packaging of the product in small sachets is also an innovation: they are convenient to store over long periods of time and thus can be kept for emergency use or consumers can buy many without it being cumbersome.

To supply PuR on a sustainable basis, P&G has explored three separate complementary models, all of them founded on a market-based approach which uses broad collaborations involving the local entrepreneurs, governments, NGOs and research institutions in order to provide effective education, marketing and product distribution:

- *a social model*, in some countries this model may be most appropriate due to economic and infrastructure constraints that limit the commercial model. The social model involves the use of established social marketing distribution channels by non-profit organizations as well as a social network approach with local NGOs and Ministries of Health;
- *a commercial model*, that leverages the technology innovation and distribution and marketing infrastructure of the private sector, combined with advocacy, education and research efforts by collaborating groups to build awareness of the need to properly treat and store water. This model is being explored in initial commercial test markets that were conducted in Guatemala, the Philippines, Morocco and Pakistan. Specific activities include a scientific symposium and outreach to build awareness, local training sessions involving village health workers;
- *an emergency relief model*, that involves product distribution along with education materials, typically by a relief agency. Several NGOs, including the International Rescue Committee and the International Committee of the Red Cross are evaluating the combination system for use in emergency situations. Simple education materials in multiple languages have been developed for the combination system to allow for rapid deployment.

4.1.5 Social and Economic Analysis

Costing $10 million to develop, PuR has provided more than 3 billion liters of purified drinking water in more than 60 countries since its introduction.

Moreover, under the brand PuR and the water filtration technologies, P&G has developed a range of products whose purchasing sustains the Children's Safe Drinking Water program. This program is the focal philanthropic program of P&G's overall cause program, P&G's Live, Learn, and Thrive TM initiative which was launched in 2004, when P&G partnered with a diverse network of organizations to create, providing awareness of this significant global issue and enabling others to help solve this problem.

From the economic point of view the analysis refers to profits derives from commercial model and indirect benefits derives from social model (e.g., brand image, brand awareness).

4.1.6 Monitoring and Evaluation

Since the launch of the product in 2003, numerous studies have been developed, in particular by the partners involved, in order to monitor and evaluate social and economic impact. Referring to social impact assessment, the results of two main studies are summarized below:

- *World Vision's final report on Midzemba Area Development Programme School Safe Water Project, August 2008*. The project was initiated in October, 2007 to assist 5,944 students in 11 primary schools and 27,000 people in 31 surrounding villages. The project goal is to reduce diarrhoea prevalence and absenteeism in targeted schools through treatment of drinking water using Water Guard WA Ufa (WGWU) from October 2007 to September 2008. The Mid-Term Evaluation had two objectives, which are to quantify the reduction in diarrhoea prevalence and to quantify reduction of absenteeism due to diarrhoea in the targeted schools. The outcome of mid-term evaluation will assist in re-planning and aligning interventions to attain the project goal. The study tools used were questionnaire, observations and focus group discussions. The report uses 13 indictors (e.g., school enrolment, general absenteeism rate, absenteeism due to diarrhoea, Coverage for making water "safe" for drinking in schools).
- International Medical Corp's final report on The Gateway Initiative: Sensitizing Children to Promote Healthy Behaviors and Families, November 2008. The program goal was to decrease incidence of water-borne diseases in households in eastern Democratic Republic of Congo in the period September 15, 2007–September 15, 2008. International Medical Corps implemented intensive monitoring and evaluation activities to assess the change in knowledge, attitudes, and behaviors towards water sanitation and hygiene practices over the course of the project. International Medical Corps surveyed 203 families.

4.1.7 Scaling Up

PuR established sustainable markets in Pakistan, Kenya, Uganda, Haiti and the Dominican Republic. PuR was also successfully used for disaster relief in many countries including Bangladesh, Zimbabwe, Sudan, Ethiopia, Iraq and in the tsunami ravaged region of South East Asia.

P&G is still working to get PuR into the market in a sustainable way, learning where to set up franchise models, and studying how to create a viable micro enterprise model to distribute a single sachet product like PuR.

Basing on its filtration technologies and know how P&G developed new product useful to water purification they sell in traditional markets (e.g., PuR Mineralclear, PuR Classicclear).

4.2 Plumpy'nut by Nutriset

4.2.1 Overview

Created in 1986, Nutriset has since remained true to its initial commitment: to invent, produce and make accessible solutions for the treatment and prevention of malnutrition.

At the time, no specific product existed for the management of severe acute malnutrition. Food aid, based on agricultural surpluses from developed countries, did not meet the nutritional requirements of young children. Michel Lescanne, a food processing engineer, founded Nutriset with the aim of finding nutritional solutions suitable for children and their living conditions.

Understanding how to guarantee the treatment of millions of children suffering from severe acute malnutrition in regions marked by a chronic lack of resources (healthcare infrastructures, human resources, funding) was the challenge that, in 1996, led Nutriset and IRD to invent Plumpy'nut, the first ready-to-use product for the treatment of severe acute malnutrition (Ready-to-Use Therapeutic Food or RUTF).

Nutriset's R&D department is composed by two main division: External Research and Nutritional Strategies Division (RESN) and Internal Research and Development Division (RDI).

RESN is tasked with proposing nutritional solutions meeting the specific needs of vulnerable communities around the globe and tailored to the conditions in which these products are used on the ground.

The Internal Research and Development Division (RDI) is responsible for product development. The ultimate aim is the manufacture of an appetizing product that can be manufactured on an industrial scale.

4.2.2 Idea Generation

The first Nutriset attempt toward a product able to face the problem of severe acute malnutrition in developing word was the development of F-100 and F-75 therapeutic milks in ready-to-dilute form, making the work of medical teams easier.

The use of F-100 and F-75 milks reduced the risks linked to getting the dosage of the different ingredients wrong. It also made it easier to implement a new protocol improving the management of patients and their chances of recovery, leading to a reduction in the mortality rates recorded in nutritional programs. But neither F-75 nor F-100 were able to overcome the main constraints related to the management of severe acute malnutrition in developing countries: the need for drinking water, the very short shelf-life of therapeutic milks once reconstituted. Moreover F-100 and F-75 need to be dispensed under medical supervision. Thus, children need to be hospitalized for several weeks at a time jointly with their mothers. These conditions represent other limits to the effectiveness of F-100 and F-75 products on the treatment of the severe malnutrition. The lack of infrastructures (hospitals, clinics with in-patient beds) and qualified human resources drastically limited the number of children treated. Additionally, very often the mothers were in no position to stay away from home for such an extended period of time. Starting from these challenges, a new product, called Pumply'nut, was developed in 1996. Plumpy'nut is the result of joint work by the Nutriset team and Dr. André Briend, a nutritionist working with the IRD (Institut de Recherche pour le Dévelopement). Plumpy'nut was the first ready-to-use food (RUTF) and helped change the face of treatment of severe acute malnutrition.

4.2.3 Testing

In 1997 in Chad, a first trial conducted on a small number of children by Action Contre la Faim in collaboration with the Chad Ministry for Health demonstrated the good acceptability of the product. In 1998 Médecins Sans Frontières (MSF) used it during a food crisis in Southern Sudan, achieving good results.

In 2000 the NGO Concern Worldwide experienced non-hospital management of cases of severe acute malnutrition in Ethiopia using Plumpy'nut. On the basis of this experiment, the article by Steve Collins, a physician specialising in nutrition, published in August 2001 in the prestigious scientific journal The Lancet, sketched out the basic principles for a community-based model for the management of severe acute malnutrition (CMAM - Community-based management of severe acute malnutrition).

In 2007, joint statement by the World Health Organization (WHO), the World Food Programme (WFP), UNICEF and the United Nations Standing Committee on Nutrition (SCN) approved the CMAM model and the use of RUTF.

4.2.4 Marketing Plan

From a product perspective Plumpy'nut represents an evolution of the F-100 product. It has the same nutritional value of the latter but requires no preparation (i.e. no dilution, no cooking). It is ready to eat, from the pot or sachet in which it is packaged, and able to be kept for 24 months after the date of manufacture and for up to 24 h after opening.

Because of these characteristics it can also be distributed out of the hospitals. Community-based Management of Acute Malnutrition (CMAM) program is the most common way to supply Plumpy'nut. This new therapeutic model, which is managed by UN agencies in collaboration with NGO's and Public health system, is based on a screening on a community level which significantly improved families' access to treatment and increased the coverage rate of malnutrition management. According to the CMAM approach, children suffering from severe acute malnutrition (determined by their height for weight ratio and mid-upper arm circumference), and who have no medical complications and still have some appetite, are qualified for home-based treatment. A mother is given a determined quantity of Plumpy'nut packets to administer to her child and must bring him back to the clinic for a weekly visit to check weight gain and make sure that the child has not become sick and, finally, obtain further supplies of RUTF.

This method has helped increase the number of children treated tenfold, at the same time relieving pressure on hospitals to allow them to concentrate on the most serious cases.

In order to satisfy the growing demand of RUTF and make them available for more people as possible, in 2005, Nutriset began developing networks of local manufacturers located as close as possible to users, by creating the Plumpy'nut in the Field network, since renamed PlumpyField. The PlumpyField network now includes manufacturing partners in developing countries as well as a no profit organization based in the United States, Edesia. Drawing inspiration from the franchise model, PlumpyField is a guarantee of quality, fostering the establishment of sustainable production systems in developing countries.

4.2.5 Social and Economic Analysis

In almost 25 years, Nutriset has firmly established itself as the world leader in treatment and prevention of malnutrition because of its ability to innovate, its mastery of high-quality production, and its commitment to make products accessible.

Under the know-how of RUTF products, Nutriset developed a wide range of Plumpy'nut products able to address moderate acute malnutrition.

Since Plumpy'nut was developed, over 5 million people have received products from the Plumpy-type products.

From an economic perspective, the creation of the Plumpy'field network makes Nutriset able to improve its production capacities. From a social perspective Plumpy'field generates a lot of benefits for the community: the introduction of the local manufacture of Plumpy' range products not only improves the response to nutritional emergencies, makes it easier to tackle chronic malnutrition outside emergency periods but, also, boosts local economies—including raw material production sectors—and fosters the incorporation of ready-to-use nutritional supplements in national nutrition strategies.

4.2.6 Monitoring and Evaluation

The External Research and Nutritional Strategies Division RESN Division was also responsible for selecting, setting up and monitoring research partnerships with external parties (universities, humanitarian organizations, public health players).

To address the huge challenge represented by malnutrition (68 million cases of acute malnutrition worldwide, 195 million children suffering from delayed growth), Nutriset deploys synergistic resources with the aim of contributing to nutritional autonomy:

- substantial investment in research and innovation in order to find ever more effective nutritional solutions. Currently the company is participating in more than 60 research projects in the world led by university or operational partners;
- development of local networks to enable high-quality nutritional solutions to be produced on field, over a sustained period of time, close to the populations requiring them. The networks participate in the economic development of the regions where they are established through job creation and the market they offer for high-quality local agriculture;
- operational communication actions relating to the products in order to make them more acceptable, taking into account the cultural characteristics of target populations;
  innovation in terms of distribution strategies, with the introduction of preventive products to the private market alongside continued cooperation with humanitarian and welfare organizations;
- constant dialogue with the players involved in nutrition and humanitarian aid, to improve the fit between our nutritional solutions and real requirements through feedback from the field;
- support for initiatives fostering greater mobilization against malnutrition (participation in the Scaling-up Nutrition action plan);
  investment in training: in addition to specific training for PlumpyField network team members, Nutriset also supports training programs in Africa (2iE engineering school, based in Ouagadougou; Programme de Leadership Africa in en Nutrition (PLAN); funding of grants for students from African countries).

4.3 Shokti Doi by Grameen Danone

4.3.1 Overview

With around 13 billion euros of total sales in 2005 (around US $15.5 million), Groupe Danone is the world leader in Fresh Dairy Products and Bottled Water (in terms of volumes), and joint world leader in the Biscuits market. 50 % of Groupe Danon's 90,000 employees work in Asia Pacific and Danone operates around 100 factories in this part of the world.

Danone is what is called a "glocal" company, in other words it is both global (thereby benefiting from economies of scale) and local (since its unit of operation is adapted to its surroundings). The business unit is the subsidiary, established in any country which functions for local consumers. Danone is therefore "glocal", but in the first place it is local, and then global.

In 1996, when Franck Riboud became president of Danone, he changed the focus of company's activity abandoning the packaging activities and developing a mission to bring good health to the greatest number of people by an appropriate diet.

Grameen Bank is the institution which gave micro credit to the world. It serves 5.8 million borrowers, 96 per cent women, representing as many families. Borrowers own the bank. It lends over half a billion dollars a year in loans averaging $120, without any collateral, or legal instruments. The bank lends for income generating purposes, for housing, for higher education of the children of the borrowers. It lends to beggars without interest. Its deposit base is larger than the loan outstanding.

Franck Riboud and Mohamed Yunus met in Paris at the end of October 2005. Following their meeting, they decided to explore the possibility of establishing a partnership in Bangladesh.

This unique initiative is intended to combine Groupe Danone's expertise in the field of healthy foods with that of the Grameen Group, set up by the founder of the Grameen Bank, a specialist in micro-credit for the poor and economic development.

The Grameen Group and Groupe Danone entered into a 50-50 joint venture agreement effective March 16th 2006, to form a company called the Grameen Danone Foods Social Business Enterprise in Bangladesh.

The four main objectives of Grameen Danone Foods Ltd.(GDFL) are as follows:

- to offer a product with high added nutritional value;
- to create jobs;
- to protect the environment;
- to be economically viable.

In mid-July, Grameen Danone acquired a plot of land in Bogra on which to build its first plant.

4.3.2 Idea Generation

Bangladesh is the second lowest country in South Asia. The index of underweight children under the age of five, which is one of the key index to monitor the human development, shows 48 %. They also lack access to healthy living conditions. These figure indicate that Bangladeshi children under the age of five are in the poorest health not only in South Asia but also in the whole world.

In order to find a n innovative solution to fight malnutrition in Bangladesh, Experts from the corporate world analyzed the market en put in evidence its characteristics.

Bangladesh is a country of insufficient energy supply, where the spread of electricity on the grid is slow and only 30 % of the population has access to it.

In this contest the primary objective of Bogra factory was to launch a dairy product at a highly affordable price in compliance with the environmental and social resources.

The expertise of Danone was useful to project the plant which was operated by solar and biogas energy.

The product should be specially developed to meet the specific nutritional needs of Bangladeshi children, guaranteeing them harmonious growth whilst providing them with all the benefits of milk and the micronutrients they lack.

A new nutritional formula was set up and integrated in a yogurt named Shokti Doi (Yogurt for power). A single 80 g pot will provide 30 % of a child's daily requirements of vitamin A, iron, zinc and iodine.

The option of a Yogurt was not a case. Yogurt does not only represent the product for which Danone is famous the world over but it is also a traditional snack in Bangladesh. Moreover yogurt is a natural dairy product filled with calcium and protein, both essential nutrients that many Bangladeshis lack.

4.3.3 Testing

In order to facilitate the diffusion of the Shokti Doi yogurt, Danone had to make sure of its taste. Thus, a trial recipe was developed and taste tests begun been conducted. Representative members of the final target audience were chosen—mother and children from the Bogra district- and teams of researchers were sent into their homes during the spring of 2006 to sample their reactions.

The initial results were not positive. Because of the fortifying ingredients the yogurt did not taste good, so the Danone flavor expert set to work to modify the formula.

The yogurt's pack and name were tasted too. Firstly a survey about the most popular animals among children was conducted by Grameen. Secondly a test about the whole marketing concept was conducted sending researchers into the villages showing sample plastic cups.

4.3.4 Marketing Plan

The marketing strategy developed for the Grameen Danone (GD) project is completely different from the traditional strategies used to market consumer good.

GDFL favors the use of ingredients available locally for several reasons: cost reduction in terms of raw materials (no import fees, simplified logistics), minimization of fossil energy consumption (reduced transportation), and to promote local community development and fight against rural exodus. Thus, GDFL faces several issues. The market for milk, main ingredient of the Shokti Doi, is very informal in Bangladesh. The cost of milk is critical for GDFL and determines the sustainability of the firm's business model. To avoid coming into competition with other milk purchasers, and so as to limit any increases in already high milk prices, GDFL had to structure the upstream market. It chose to develop micro-farms to form part of its own supply network. Micro-credits are offered by the Grameen Bank to potential owners of dairy cattle, who receive a guaranteed annual fixed price and veterinary advice which helps to improve quality and output. The same channel structure has been created for date molasses, the natural date tree syrup, which is much cheaper than sugar and very appreciated by local populations for its strong flavor.

The informal network of main markets and door–to-door sales people is by far the most developed in Bangladesh (supermarkets are mainly located in rich neighborhoods of Dhaka, the capital city, and some small stores exist in more densely populated zones). Thus, GDFL had to find an alternative to its conventional retail distribution. Door to door sales are ensured by the "Grameen Ladies". Although illiterate, these women are trained to deliver a nutritional message and receive a commission for each yogurt they sell; they are not employees of GDFL and their unsold items are not taken back.

As well as door to door distribution, Shokti Doi is also sold in existing stores which offer an array of products, mostly food products.

The yogurt was priced well below the market price for unfortified yogurts in Bangladesh, making it more affordable for low-income consumers. Its price has been set at 5 BDT per 80 g portion, around 6 Euro cents, so that even the poorest Bangladeshi families will be able to afford to buy it regularly.

Shokti Doi means Yogurt for Power. It was a good name, which captured the benefits of the nutrients that fortify the yogurt.

To promote the use of the yogurt among children an attractive symbol like a friendly animal should be associated to it. Between a monkey, a tiger and a lion, the latter was chosen to become the Shokti Doi testimonial. Monkeys were not aligned with the concept of power and tigers were already used for product promotion.

To reduce the environmental impact generated by its activities, Grameen Danone has decided to manufacture the pots in which Shokti Doi is sold using a recyclable material.

The pots will be made using PLA (Poly Lactic Acid) which is created from corn starch, and is therefore 100 % biodegradable at certain temperatures and humidity levels.

To degrade the residues from the PLA used in the plant, a bio-digester has been installed at the Grameen Danone plant in Bogra. It will produce biogas (mixture of CO_2 and methane), which will then be recovered and used for various heating and lighting purposes.

Due to the lack of conventional media, the standard advertisement model (press and television based ad campaigns) had to be questioned. GDFL was fortunate to get the support of Zinedine Zidane, the internationally famous French soccer player, who visited the factory and contributed to a spectacular brand launch.

With the support of GAIN (Global Alliance for Improved Nutrition) Grameen Danone's nutritional messages were defined:

- informative posters were displayed inside the meeting centers used by Grameen Bank borrowers groups (every week, around 160,000 women meet at these centers, offering a fantastic window for reaching out to potential consumers),

- the Grameen Ladies distributing Shokti Doi carried a visual aid explaining the product's health benefits,
- educational games were handed out at schools in the Bogra area. This provided a fun way for children to learn that a balanced diet goes hand in hand with physical and intellectual development.

4.3.5 Social and Economic Analysis

The production of yogurt by Grameen Danone has improved people's quality of life in Bogra because of its nutritional profit and employment profit.

Shokti Doi naturally contains calcium and proteins, essential elements for bone strength and growth, and it is also enriched in micronutrients. A container of 80 grams provides 30 percent of a child's daily nutritional needs in vitamin A, iron, zinc and salt. Its live cultures also reduce the intensity and length of diarrhea. Shokti Doi should have a strong nutritional impact on children aged 3 to 15 who eat it on a regular basis.

Local people, including Grameen borrowers, have already started new jobs or expanded business opportunities as well as gotten employment opportunities. the Bangladesh-based company employs 50 people at its Bogra plant, which within 1 year of its launch already produces 10,000 servings of Shokti Doi yogurt a day.

A door-to-door distribution system has created jobs for 300 women in the rural area around the factory, and 400 farmers supply milk for its production line at a guaranteed price.

Concerning the profit equation, Grameen Danone is a company keen to respect the lines of conduct set down by the mission, concerning the creation of a «social busi-ness enterprise».

This does not mean that Grameen Danone must be a loss-making company, but rather that the profits it makes will be reinvested to develop new businesses.

Moreover there are a lot of intangibles benefits which impact on Danone profitability. Firstly, Through this partnership Danone found nutrition experts who specialized in the needs of developing.

countries, an area where Danone lacked expertise. Secondly the company improve its reputation and finally it obtains free access in new potential market.

4.3.6 Monitoring and Evaluation

Between 2008 and 2011, the Global Alliance for Improved Nutrition (GAIN) funded a study conducted by Johns Hopkins Bloomberg School of Public Health, to evaluate the impact of fortified yogurt on the nutritional status and cognitive performance of school-aged children in Bangladesh. The yogurt, produced by Grameen Danone Foods, was supplied during 1 year to school children aged 6 to

9 years in the town of Gabtali in Bogra District, where Grameen Danone Foods has a factory. Every day, the children were fed one cup (60 g) of the fortified yogurt to help meet their daily vitamin A, iron, zinc and iodine requirements.

Preliminary findings, which have been presented at the 2011 XI Asian Congress of Nutrition in Bangkok, Thailand, showed that micronutrient-fortified yogurt had a positive impact on children's growth rate in terms of height. Computerized tests also revealed improved capacity of children to concentrate and learn.

4.3.7 Scaling Up

Grameen Danone Foods is the danone.communities' first project. In 2008, the French Risk Mutual Fund (FCPR) danone.communities will provide financing to enable Grameen Danone to raise production capacity at Bogra and build a second factory near Dhaka.

Other initiatives are also being studied in Asia and Africa. These will involve partnerships based on the original business model, combining Groupe Danone's expertise with that of local entities or NGOs.

The danone.communities project also aims to build a large community of a new kind of investors. All partners share a commitment to linking finance and sustainable development, the belief that the priority for projects is their social impact, and the conviction that such projects must be profitable for this impact to be lasting.

4.4 Interceptor by BASF

4.4.1 Overview

BASF is the world's leading chemical company. Its portfolio ranges from chemicals, plastics and performance products to agricultural products, fine chemicals as well as oil and gas.

With about 111,000 employees, six Verbund sites and close to 370 production sites worldwide we serve customers and partners in almost all countries of the world.

Within its Agriculture division, There is the BASF's Public Health business sector which responsible for improving the quality of life for people in developing nations around the globe through disease prevention by working with the international community, including international health, government and humanitarian organizations, to provide innovative vector control products and programs.

For decades, BASF has been committed to the fight against malaria and other tropical diseases and in 2006 BASF launched an innovative product called Interceptor.

4.4.2 Idea Generation

Malaria is one of last three major epidemic diseases, killing well over a million people a year. Only AIDS and tuberculosis claim more victims. Malaria is caused by tiny single-celled organisms called plasmodia transmitted by mosquitoes of the Anopheles genus. Ninety percent of these cases are concentrated in Africa, with young children being most affected. Every 30 s a child dies of malaria in Africa and almost every second victim is under five.

According with WHO statement, Vector control is the primary public health intervention for reducing malaria transmission at the community level. It is the only intervention that can reduce malaria transmission from very high levels to close to zero. A simple, uncoated mosquito nets were not able to face the fight against malaria. Moreover, conventionally insecticide treated nets have the disadvantage of losing their insecticidal activity after just a few months. The WHO therefore asked the chemical industry to develop nets only treating the net with an insecticide that is safe for humans really puts the insects out of action.

In 2006, Putting together its expertise in textile development and insect control, Basf produced Interceptor, a special long lasting mosquito net.

BASF already had access to the ideal active ingredient: alphacypermethrin. As the active ingredient in the insecticide Fendona, it already has a long history of use in BASF crop protection and global health products.

Alphacypermethrin is modeled on the natural defensive compound produced by chrysanthemums and kills insects even in the smallest doses. For vertebrates, and thus for humans, the amount used on the nets is not toxic

In the nets' production, a polymer binder system is combined with Fendona insecticide and applied directly to the fibers of the nets in a unique treatment process. Fendona, based on the active ingredient alpha-cypermethrin, is slowly released and rapidly knocks down, kills or repels mosquitoes as they come into contact with the net. This controlled release of the insecticide ensures long-term effectiveness and the net delivers its protection even after 20 washes. The system also ensures the nets are odorless, soft to the touch and pleasant to sleep under. This is important to ensure that the nets are used.

4.4.3 Testing

The new product was tested for effectiveness at the London School of Hygiene & Tropical Medicine. The researchers found that in most cases even brief contact with the net is sufficient to seal a mosquito's fate.

The laboratory test was followed by different field test. Starting from 2010 Interceptor had been tested in India, Libanon and Uganda achieving good result all the time.

4.4.4 Marketing Plan

The main customers for the Interceptor net, which costs only a few dollars, are international aid organizations, national health agencies and nongovernmental organizations, which usually purchase the nets in large public tenders or fund countries for local tenders.

In order to answer to the WHO expectation (The total demand is likely to reach 50 to 60 million nets annually in the years ahead), BASF has established production capacities to supply a good portion of the demand. Recently new factories have already been founded in emerging countries to promote and increase the use of long lasting mosquito nets.

4.4.5 Social and Economic Analysis

From a social perspective, insecticide treated nets have shown to be able to lower malaria transmission by 90 %. Moreover, because the net is long-lasting, it is highly cost-effective as well as being user-friendly. No dipping. No re-treatment. No mess. No fuss.

From a company perspective, BASF has been recognized for its commitment to furthering the critical mission of worldwide sustainability and social responsibility. Moreover Basf is a founding member of the United Nations Global Compact and Global Compact LEAD, a new platform established in 2011 for corporate sustainability leadership, BASF has also been recognized by the Dow Jones Sustainability World Index for ten consecutive years.

4.4.6 Monitoring and Evaluation

In some area mosquito are already becoming resistant to existing solutions. In 2010, BASF has signed an agreement with the London School of Hygiene & Tropical Medicine (LSHTM) and the Innovative Vector Control Consortium (IVCC) to develop a new generation of malaria prevention products based on the BASF insecticide chlorfenapyr.

4.4.7 Scaling Up

When interceptor was launched in 2007, the first market was Africa. Even now Africa detains the highest request of long lasting mosquito nets but, at the same time, other markets like Latin America and Asia.

Moreover other classical BASF's product were associated to the nets in the fighting against malaria: indoor residual spraying to reduce the survival of vectors entering houses or sleeping areas and larvicides to treat standing water.

Finally in order to satisfy the market request and achieve new target, Basf introduce a new production site in Asia. In 2008, Grameen Healthcare Trust and BASF (Germany) got together and created BASF Grameen Ltd.

BASF Grameen Limited can source from a local production plant located in Social Business Industrial Park in Sarabo. The plant owned by Grameen Fabrics & Fashions Limited was inaugurated on March 23, 2012. It manufactures long lasting insecticide impregnated nets) under the brand name Interceptor. These nets will be marketed by BASF Grameen Limited and all the profit, after covering its own costs and recouping the partners' initial investment, should be reinvested fully in the company.

Appendix
Research Methodology

In order to identify the main critical success factors in social product innovation process (Chap. 3) an empirical analysis was carried out on four social products developed by four different companies:

- PuR by Procter and Gamble;
- Plumpy'nut by Nutriset;
- Shokti Doi by Grameen Danone Food;
- Interceptor by BASF Grameen.

The research, mainly descriptive in nature (Woodside and Wilson 2003; Eisenhardt 1989) is based on the multiple-case (holistic) model (Yin 2003), and the single product has been considered as the analysis unit. According to Eisenhardt (1989) framework, the research process has been structured in seven steps: selecting cases, crafting instruments and protocols, entering the field, analyzing data, shaping hypothesis, enfolding literature and reaching closure.

In the first stage of the research (case selection) PuR (Procter and Gamble), Plumpy'nut (Nutriset), Shokti Doi (Grameen Danone Food) and Interceptor (BASF Grameen) where selected for at least four reasons.

Firstly, all the companies are dedicated to identify, develop and use leading technologies in different sectors (health care, nutrition and chemical).

Secondly, they have been widely recognised for being socially engaged towards environmental and social community. Thirdly, social innovations are addressed to developing countries and the new products have had positive social impact that has been widely recognized at international level. Lastly, the author had the possibility to access confidential information.

In the second step (crafting instruments and protocols) the information was gathered using documentary materials both internal (e.g., presentations, reports, etc.) and external (e.g., websites, press releases, publications, etc.). Documentary evidences are considered objectives because they are generated outside the influence of the researcher (Johnston et al. 1999).

In the third step data were coded using the framework proposed based on the following categories of analysis: idea generation, testing, marketing plan and monitoring.

L. Michelini, *Social Innovation and New Business Models*, SpringerBriefs in Business,
DOI: 10.1007/978-3-642-32150-4,

In order to increase the degree of the research's validity (Riege 2003), a grid to organise the information have been produced to analyse the cases (e.g., internal validity), (Miles and Huberman 1994).

In the phase data analysis the entire documentary materials collected was evaluated by two different researchers independently. Each researcher conducted the data coding independently using the same categories of analysis. Than the research team compared and discussed findings.

The phase of shaping hypotheses was focused on building evidence which had to measure the construct in each case as well as to verify that "the emergent relationships between constructs fit with the evidence in each case" (Eisenhardt 1989, p. 542). After having accumulated data from different documents, the researchers verified each category of each case.

In order to increase the degree of external validity of the analysis, in the step of enfolding literature, the results were analysed and compared with the literature (Yin 2003) and in the last stage (reaching closure) the main research propositions were defined.

References

Eisenhardt K (1989) Building theories from case study research. Acad Manag Rev 4:532–550

Johnston W J, Leach MP, Liu AH (1999) Theory testing using case studies in business-to-business research. Ind Market Manag 28(3):201–213

Miles MB, Huberman AM (1994) Qualitative data analysis: an expanded source-book. Sage Publications (2nd edn), Newbury Park, California

Riege AM (2003) Validity and Reliability tests in case study research: a literature review with hands-on applications for each research phase. Qual Mark Res Intern J 2:75–86

Woodside AG, Wilson EJ (2003) Case study research methods for theory building. J Bus Ind Mark 6/7:493–508

Yin RK (2003) Case study research. Sage publications, 3rd (Edn), Newbury Park, California

The manufacturer's authorised representative in the EU is Springer Nature Customer Service Centre GmbH, Europaplatz 3, 69115 Heidelberg, Germany. If you have any concerns regarding our products, please contact ProductSafety@springernature.com

Printed and bound by CPI Group (UK) Ltd, Croydon, CR0 4YY
30/09/2026
02225606-0009